NEW REVISED EDITION

HORSEBACK RIDING

by
Sheila Wall

Photographs by Ted Freudy

Published by
Melvin Powers
WILSHIRE BOOK COMPANY
12015 Sherman Road
No. Hollywood, California 91605
Telephone: (213) 875-1711

Acknowledgments

So many people gave generously of their time and advice that it is impossible to adequately express my gratitude. However, I would like to give particular thanks to

my sister, Ann Wall Miller, without whose editorial and secretarial skills this book would never have been written;

my father, Joseph J. Wall, who taught me to ride, for his constructive criticism;

Stuart Rose, for his encouragement and invaluable advice;

Miss Connie Barnes, who so skillfully and patiently posed for the majority of the photographs;

Miss Sandra Stokes, Miss Deborah Lynn King, Mr. Richard D. Abbott and Miss Alexandra L. Hanna who kindly gave of their riding talent in the additional pictures taken for this new edition;

Adrian Bronk, who covered the countryside to get "on the spot" photographs;

Col. and Mrs. Howard C. Fair for their information on the Pony Club;

Mrs. J. Austin du Pont, Rear Adm. and Mrs. Lester Hundt, Mr. Milton Erlanger, Mr. Rodman Wanamaker, Dr. M. Phyllis Lose, Mrs. Frank Rhodes, Mrs. Henry Elser and Mrs. Rowland Windsor, for kindly permitting photographs to be taken of their horses and farms;

Millard Heller, Alex and Richard Atkinson, for their unfailing help and advice through the years;

Gregory Goff, Sandra Randall, Michael Wall, Anne Hanna, Mary Ann Richards, Carol Lankford, Susan Hosford, Nancy Meisenhelter, the McCauley family, Pat Ridgeway, Alice Dickey, Christopher Elser, and Carol Heller (and their parents), for their participation in the photographs;

Photographs by Ted Freudy.

To My Father and Mother

Contents

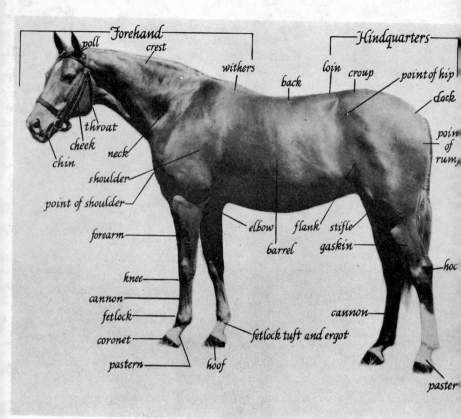

Chapter I

Riding Is Fun...

Would you like to show, hunt, ride in horse trials or race? Or do you want to know just enough about horses to take a quiet ride through the countryside? Whatever your aims are in riding, the more you know about the sport the more you will enjoy it. Riding horses has fascinated people through the ages because there is always something to learn, there is always a new horse to ride and every horse is different.

Every time you get on a horse consider it a challenge, a chance for you and your horse to correct a bad habit, improve an old skill or learn something new. Don't become discouraged because you have trouble learning something or because your horse misbehaves. Anyone who really wants to, can ride well. It will take time—you cannot learn everything at once—and it will take work, but the fundamentals are fun.

Most people can stay on a horse at a walk, trot and canter after a few lessons. But the better your form and the greater your understanding of your horse, the more confident you will be and the more readily your horse will respond to your commands. Good horsemanship means good fun; better horsemanship means more fun.

What is a horse? Around forty-five million years ago "Eohippus," the dawn-horse, evolved in the Rocky Mountains of North America. You would not have recognized him as the ancestor of the modern horse. He wasn't much bigger than a good-sized tom cat. In fact, he looked a great deal like a cat; you could have picked him up with one hand. He had a short neck, padded feet and small teeth. How did he survive at this time just after the dinosaurs and giant reptiles dominated the earth? His active brain and remarkable legs helped him to outwit and outrun his enemies. In fact, the word "horse" stems from an Icelandic word meaning "to run."

As the number of horses increased, they traveled to South America and over the land bridge to Asia, Africa and Europe. In South America about 500,000 B.C., a strange disease wiped out not only all the horses but the camels, tigers and elephants as well. With the coming of the great glacial masses, the horse was pushed out of North America.

The horse grew in size slowly as the eons passed. Gradually he developed a more streamlined shape for greater speed, a longer neck for better balance, and a larger jaw with more effective teeth for grazing. He lost all his toes but one; its nail developed into the modern hoof.

The horse was not tall enough to carry a grown man comfortably when man discovered this animal could be put to better uses than supplying an occasional meal. Other animals tasted better and the horse was easily trained to do a variety of tasks. By the second century B.C., the horse was an important part of man's life. He pulled chariots, tilled the land and carried man on his travels and in his wars. By the first century B.C. horses were being used for sport. In the twenty-third Olympiad in Greece chariot races were held. References to horses are found in the religious legends of the peoples from India to Germany centuries before Christ.

When the Moslems invaded Spain in the eighth century after Christ, they brought with them herds of their speedy, intelligent Arabian horses and bred them to the somewhat heavier native stock. In northern Europe the horses were being bred for their size and strength, to carry knights and their heavy load of armor. These horses were the ancestors of our draft breeds, such as the Percheron and Clydesdale. Later, during the wars with Spain and during the Crusades, the knights found themselves outmaneuvered by faster, lighter horses. Wisely they crossed their own horses with these lighter breeds to gain greater speed and effectiveness.

With the arrival of the Spanish explorers in the sixteenth century, the horse returned to the land of his birth, America. Some of these horses were lost; others strayed and formed bands of wild mustangs. In the late seventeenth and early eighteenth centuries the Byerly Turk, Godolphin Arabian and Darley Arabian were brought to England. These Oriental stallions were bred successfully with English mares. All thoroughbreds descend from them. Eventually, many thoroughbreds were brought across the ocean. Here in America the standardbred, Morgan, walking horse and quarter horse were developed from them.

Watch sleek race horses testing their speed, or pony foals frolicking in a field. Think of what a long way the horse has come since the time of Eohippus, the dawn-horse. Notice too that the horse's greatest assets are still the same—swift legs and an alert brain.

So you want to ride? This book will tell you the basic principles. Learn them well and you will not have to retrace your steps when you go on to more advanced riding. But no book can show you how to ride. Lessons are invaluable. Your instructor can pinpoint your particular faults, correct your position and help you over those first rough spots. Your lessons and your book will work together to make you a good rider.

If the cost of lessons from a professional is beyond your means, don't give up. You may be able to earn them. Rare is the stable that cannot use some extra help. Then, too, you will be surprised how many people are willing to help beginners with their riding and the care of their horses. Experienced riders both young and old, particularly those connected with your local hunt club, are usually generous with their time and knowledge.

The Junior Cavalry of America has been a great aid to young riders. At the moment the only troops not associated with prep schools are located in New Canaan, Connecticut (headquarters), and in Essex, New Jersey. Perhaps you and your friends can start a troop in your area. The Junior Cavalry is a non-profit organization and the size of the fees paid by a cadet depend on the cost of the running of the unit. Through the medium of organized riding this dedicated group "strives to teach the individual to put aside his own desires when they conflict with what is best for the group; to obey quickly and cheerfully and to undertake responsibility." The cadet maxim is: "It is never the fault of the horse when something goes wrong; it's always the rider. Improve your own skill and you will be able to ride every horse successfully." The cadet's goal is: "To get the best performance from each mount with the least effort on the part of both rider and horse." The Junior Cavalry's method of teaching riding is based on that of the United States Cavalry.

However, the most widespread source of help to young riders in America today is the United States Pony Club. Organized in 1953, it now has nearly seven thousand members. If there is not one in your area, why not get one started? (See appendix.)

You don't have to ride a pony to be a member of the Pony Club. Our club is based on the British Pony Club. In the British Isles all the classes for juniors, whether they ride ponies or horses, are called pony classes—hence the name "pony" club.

Anyone can afford to join a pony club. The instruction is donated by experienced riders, veterinarians and horseshoers. If at all possible most pony clubs will arrange to lend you a mount. They will teach you horsemanship (good form and understanding of your horse) and sportsmanship (consideration for your horse and your fellow riders). The ideal of the Pony Club is: "To produce a thoroughly happy, comfortable horseman, riding across natural country, with complete confidence and perfect balance on a pony or horse equally happy and confident and free from pain or bewilderment." These should be the aims of all horsemen.

Whether you wish to ride one day a week or seven, whether you aim to jump five-foot fences or to canter through the park, you will want to develop good horsemanship. Why? Because the better your horsemanship the more fun you will have. The ingredients of good horsemanship are an understanding of horses in general and the horse you are riding in particular—plus good form. When you understand that a horse learns principally from memory, that he is a nervous and timid animal, that he is not particularly affectionate and that he can think of only one thing at a time, you are well on the way to being a good horseman as well as a good rider.

Now that you see the importance of understanding your horse, you will realize the importance of riding with good form. Through good form you can tell your horse clearly what you expect of him; you will be secure and comfortable in the saddle. Through bad form you will continually punish your horse, although you don't mean to do so.

What is good form? The principles of good form while riding cross-country are found in the principles of the forward seat. These principles are based on what is best for the horse and best for the rider. The forward seat means simply that the rider is in balance with the horse at all times.

The forward seat was discovered at the beginning of this century by Tod Sloan, an American jockey. He realized through experience that if he shortened his stirrups and leaned forward during a race, the horse could run faster. Until this time riders rode with long stirrups and sat straight or even leaned back (over fences). As Mr. Sloan continued to win races both here and in England, people realized the importance of his discovery. An officer of the Italian Cavalry worked out the theory of the forward seat over fences and the members of the Italian Cavalry practiced it with such success in international competition that riders throughout the world took it up. Thus the forward seat was developed as the best seat on a hunter or jumper and this is the seat we will talk about in this book.

Chapter II

From Grooming...

Getting ready to ride—cleaning your horse and tacking him up—need not be a chore. Rather it can be fun. Think of it as a time to get to know your horse better. Your horse enjoys being groomed properly. He responds to a thoughtful grooming just as a dog responds to petting.

To take your horse from the stall you will need a halter and a shank (lead rope). Put the halter on, making sure it is neither too tight nor too loose, and snap the shank on the round ring at the back of the halter. For proper control use a shank rather than holding the halter with your hand. Lead the horse from your right, holding the shank a few inches from the snap with your right hand and holding the end of the shank with your left so that he will not step on it. Never wrap the shank around your hand as you will be unable to release it quickly if the horse bolts or rears. Stretch your right hand out, keeping his head away from you so that he cannot step on your heels. If you face

the direction you are going, the horse will follow along behind you. You may see people facing their horse and tugging on the lead shank, unable to understand why he won't move. A horse will never step on you purposely; consequently, he won't move forward if you are in front of him.

When the halter and shank are on the horse, open the stall door wide and lead him straight through so that he does not knock his hip bones. It is important that you do not permit your horse to rush in and out of the stall, that you train him to walk quietly.

The cross-tie method is the best way to fasten your horse when you groom him. To use this method, run ropes or chains from opposite walls to each side of his halter. This will prevent him from moving around too much. If it is impossible to use the cross-tie method, tie him to a ring or post making sure that anything you tie him to is solid.

To groom a horse properly you need five tools: a currycomb, dandy (stiff) brush, soft brush, comb and hoof pick. The currycomb can be made of steel or rubber, but a rubber one is best as it is not so hard on the horse. The chief job of the currycomb is to loosen mud, sweat and dust. Use it in a circular motion, against the hair, starting up near the horse's ears and working backward. Do not use the currycomb below the knees or the hocks. This is irritating to the bones which have no fat or muscle to protect them. Be careful when using it on other places where the bone is close to the surface of the skin or where the horse is tender or ticklish.

Next use the dandy brush. This brush will lift the dirt loosened by the currycomb and will clean the heavy dirt off the legs. Put the dandy brush in your working hand, the hand closest to the horse, and the currycomb in your idle hand. In awkward places, such as inside the legs, use whichever hand is convenient. After every few strokes with your brush, clean it on the currycomb. Again start behind the ears, but now work with the hair except for any particularly stubborn spots which you can scrub. Throw your weight behind your arm if you want to get good results.

When you are cleaning the legs, pay special attention to the back of the pasterns and the heels. Mud and water collect here and are apt to cause a disease called scratches which cracks the skin and can be very painful. Some horses have such fine coats and sensitive hides that the dandy brush and currycomb are painful. Use them with discretion.

Now take your soft brush; clean the head well and polish off the rest of the horse. If there is any heavy dirt on the head you can use the dandy brush gently. Brush out the mane and tail with a dandy brush and take out any tangles with the comb. With a clean cloth wipe the eyes, nostrils and dock of the tail.

To complete the grooming, brush down the mane with a little water to keep it on the right side and polish off the whole horse with a towel. Lots of elbow grease with the brushes and towel will not only produce a gleaming horse but it will help to make a healthy one. A good grooming stimulates the circulation, aids muscle tone—and your horse loves it. In fact, in the days when soldiers were mounted on horses, they were instructed to give their mounts extra groomings when food was scarce.

To clean the front feet, stand close to the horse's shoulder with your back to his head. Pick up the leg by taking the hand

closest to it and running your thumb and forefinger down the tendon, pinching it if necessary. If the horse still won't pick up his hoof, push against his shoulder with your shoulder, making him shift his weight to his other leg. As he picks up his hoof, slide your hand around toward the toe so that the hoof rests in the palm of your hand. Take the hoof pick in your free hand and start from the toe working toward the heel. Pay special attention to the cleft on either side of the frog and the slight cleft in the middle of the frog as these are the places where a stone may be caught or where thrush may start. Thrush is the rotting of the frog and is caused by improper cleansing. You will recognize it by its odor of rot. When cleaning the clefts, be careful not to deepen them by digging too energetically with the pick.

To pick up the hind feet, stand close to the horse's hind quarters and run your hand down the inside of his leg. As he lifts his leg, pull it slightly forward. Be careful not to pull it out toward you as this will cause the horse to lose his balance and resist. To clean the hoof, ease the leg backward a bit and rest the hoof in your hand and on your inside leg between the knee and thigh. Remember that to kick with his hind leg, a horse

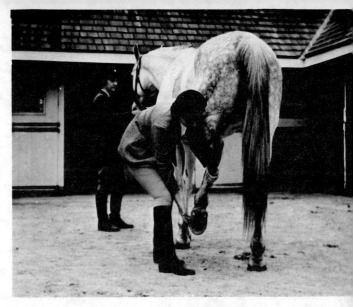

must first pull his foot forward, just as a boxer must draw his fist back to strike a blow.

Now that you have a clean horse, you are ready to "tack up." Your tack consists of a bridle, saddle and sometimes a martingale and/or breastplate. There are many different kinds of bits

Snaffle.

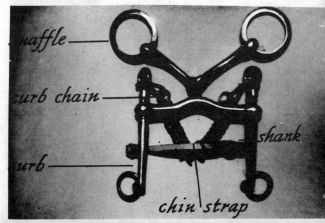

 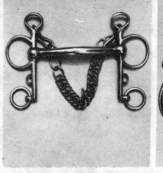 

Rubber pelham.   Steel pelham.   Kimberwick.

but they are all based on the following: snaffle, bit and bridoon (double) and pelham. One of these bits is suitable on nearly every horse so we will examine them only. The variations on these bits are used on certain horses to correct particular faults but you will not be learning to ride on "problem" horses.

The snaffle bit works chiefly on the corners of the horse's mouth. It is a mild bit and only should be used on horses with sensitive mouths. You may want to use a snaffle because one rein seems so easy to manage. But if this means a tugging contest between you and the horse, you are better off using a more severe bit. Isn't it better to use a stronger bit gently than to use a snaffle harshly?

Usually the best bit for a beginner is some sort of a pelham. A steel pelham is more severe than a rubber one and a pelham with port or a long shanked rubber pelham is more severe than the short-shanked Tom Thumb. The pelham works principally on the bars of the horse's mouth which are spaces on the lower jaw between the front and back teeth. As the steel pelham is thinner than the rubber pelham, it can dig into the tender bars of the horse's mouth. The Tom Thumb has a short shank so that less leverage is put on the bars than with a full-sized pelham

with a longer shank, or a pelham with port which acts on the tongue as well as the bars. All pelhams have curb chains which rest under the chin, catching the bars between them and the bit. The upper rein is called the snaffle rein since it acts much the same as if it were on a snaffle bit. The snaffle rein has a milder effect than the curb rein which is the lower rein. This rein, attached to the shank, has more leverage on the bars and it also brings the curb chain into action. One of these pelhams should be suitable for a beginner if he is properly mounted.

The double bridle, also called bit and bridoon or snaffle and curb, is composed of the bridoon, which is much the same as the plain snaffle only smaller, and the curb. The curb has a port (hump) in the middle so that the bit acts on the horse's tongue as well as his bars. This bit can be quite severe if used improperly and is dangerous in the hands of a beginner. You certainly wouldn't want to lean on the horse's mouth or jerk it with a double bridle.

The curb bit should never be used alone as it is too harsh on the horse's tender mouth. Not only is it cruel, but it doesn't achieve its purpose. It makes the horse want to fight rather than obey. Have you ever noticed how unhappy the horses are in the Western productions on television and in the movies? Notice how they throw their heads, roll their eyes, half rearing, hoping to escape the hurt of the long-shanked curb when they are jerked to a stop. Be considerate. Keep in mind that the gentler you are with your horse, the gentler he will be with you.

If you are wondering what bit to use on your horse, it is safer to ask an experienced person's advice than to be sorry. Remember, the bridle is there to persuade your horse to do your wishes. If you use it to force him, he will fight it and he is stronger than you are. The result will be an uncomfortable and unsafe ride.

Martingales are used to control the action of the horse's head.

If a horse carries his head properly, he does not need a martingale. The standing martingale runs from the back of the noseband, through a strap around the horse's neck which holds it in place, to the girth. This martingale is effective on horses who hold their heads too high or throw their heads.

The running martingale starts out as one strap from the girth but splits in half, each strap having a ring on the end. The snaffle reins of any bridle are put through the rings. The purpose of the running martingale is the same as the standing: to keep the horse's head where it belongs. But it achieves its end through keeping the snaffle rein in place. When a horse raises its head, thus lifting the rein out of position, he can slide the bit off the bars of his mouth. He has thus "gotten away from the bit" and it is difficult to control him as you no longer have any leverage on the jaw. The running martingale, by holding the rein down, helps hold the bit down on the bars of the mouth; the standing martingale causes the noseband to press on the horse's nose when he misbehaves.

The breastplate helps hold the saddle in position. For example, on horses with high withers or little rib expansion, it keeps the saddle from sliding backward. Martingales can be attached to breastplates.

The two basic saddles used in cross-country riding are the straight saddle and the forward seat. The forward seat saddle, with its high cantle and knee rolls, was developed particularly for forward seat riding. You will probably be happier riding in it than in a straight saddle with its flat seat and straight skirts. The parts of the saddle are the pommel, seat, cantle, skirts, possibly kneerolls, stirrups, stirrup leathers and girth. Girths are usually made of leather, either folded, sewn or plaited. With the folded girth, make sure the rounded edge is toward the horse's elbow as the open edge will pinch him.

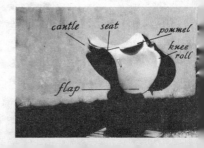

Above left: straight saddle. Note the flatter seat and the straight flap. Contour girth with elastic at one end. Above right: forward seat saddle with deeper seat and knee roll. Notice how the stirrup is pulled up on the inside of the stirrup leather and the end of the leather is slipped through the stirrup to keep it from sliding down.

knee roll

billet strap

skirt

buckle cover

Chapter III

To Tacking up...

After the horse is groomed, you are ready to tack up. Put the saddle on first while the horse is still tied. Grasping the pommel and cantle, set the saddle gently on the withers, moving it backward until it slides into position with the front padding resting in the hollow behind the shoulder blades. Always slide the saddle backward, rather than push it forward, so that the horse's hair will lie flat. Saddle sores, an irritated horse and an unpleasant ride are often caused by a badly placed saddle. Tighten the girth quickly before the horse moves, and if he does move, make sure the saddle has not slipped. Then pull each front leg up and forward in order to release any loose skin that might be caught under the girth behind the elbow.

Most horses blow their bellies out when you tighten the girth, so check the girth before you mount and again after you have walked around for a few minutes. It is easier to tighten the girth when mounted so don't worry if you cannot get it quite tight enough at first try. With the girth fastened, check that there is a width of two fingers between the pommel and the top of the withers. If the saddle presses on the withers, it will quickly cause a sore back. If you must use a saddle with a low pommel, use a pommel pad (thick-knitted pad) or a saddle cloth folded several times.

To put on the bridle, unhook the cross-ties or shank and put the reins over the horse's head. Then take off the halter. You can hold the horse with the reins if he decides to move forward. Stand on the horse's left, facing front. Put your right arm around behind his chin and hold the top of the bridle with your hand in front of his forehead. Hold the bit between the thumb and forefinger of your left hand and press it against his teeth. Most horses will automatically open their mouths but, if a horse

resists, press his lower lip over the bars with your thumb. As he opens his mouth, slip the bit in and lift the crownpiece over his far ear first and then his near ear being careful of his eyes. Pull his mane and forelock from under the crownpiece which should be lying in the hollow behind the poll. Adjust the brow band so that it does not pinch his ears. Make sure all your keepers are up and that the noseband is straight. Then buckle the throat latch, hook the curb chain and you are ready to ride.

Every part of the bridle has a particular job to do when adjusted correctly. The brow band and throat latch help keep the bridle in place. The cheek straps hold the bit. The noseband keeps the horse from opening his jaw wide enough to get away from the bit and also holds the standing martingale when used. The curb strap keeps the curb chain in place.

The brow band should be long enough so that the bridle does not pinch the horse's ears but not so long as to sag in the middle. The throat latch should be loose enough so that it will not cut the horse's breathing when he moves his head and so that his

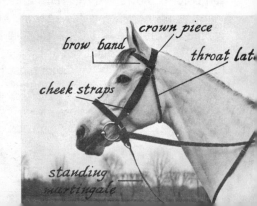

brow band • crown piece • throat lat• • cheek straps • standing martingale

windpipe can expand when he is galloping. If you can insert four fingers vertically between the horse's throat and the strap, then it is properly adjusted. The curb chain should lie flat against the horse's chin. If it is twisted it will cut the tender skin.

As you can see, adjusting the bit is important. The snaffle should be high enough to wrinkle slightly the corners of the horse's mouth. The pelham should rest on the bars, so it will be tight enough just to touch the corners of his mouth. On double bridle, the bridoon will be adjusted like the snaffle and the curb like the pelham. In other words the snaffle is on top of the curb.

Tacking up properly takes experience. Until you can feel when the saddle sits just right and until you are sure that you have the bit set properly, get an experienced person's help. It's not much fun if the horse tosses his head or pulls during your ride because the bit is annoying him. And it may be funny to see someone tumble off because the saddle has slipped under the horse's barrel, but it's not so funny if that someone is you.

"Bitting" a horse or pony, that is, selecting the proper type of bit for each horse and adjusting the bit to fit properly, is really something of an art. Experienced horsemen give it considerable thought. Even the width of a bit is a consideration. Many "bad" horses have been reclaimed by proper bitting and many promising horses have been ruined by bad bitting. However, you must start somewhere so don't be intimidated by all this. As a beginner, the bit will already have been chosen for the horse. Learn the above instructions and strive to develop light hands as quickly as possible and you need not worry. Your horse is a patient friend. He senses when you mean well and will forgive an occasional mistake.

Chapter IV

And Mounting, Dismounting...

Now that you have your horse tacked up, you will want to know how to mount properly. Just "getting aboard" could be all right were you to mount a quiet, small horse on home ground. But try the scramble technique on a green or nervous horse or when you are in the country and your horse is eager for a good canter, and you will be a horseless rider.

To mount: stand close to the horse's left shoulder. With your left hand, pick up the reins neatly, gathering them short enough to prevent the horse from moving forward. Face the horse's tail. Grasp the mane close to the saddle with your left hand or,

lacking mane, take hold of the pommel. Take hold of the far side of the stirrup with your right hand. Put your left foot in the stirrup, bracing your knee against the saddle so that you don't dig your toe into the horse's side. Grasp the cantle of the saddle with your right hand; swing up by pushing up with your right leg and lifting your body with your arms. As you swing your leg over the horse's quarters (making sure not to kick him), move your right hand to the pommel for balance and ease into the saddle.

If you are short and the horse is tall, and you can't quite reach that stirrup, don't struggle: you are not really cheating if you let down the stirrup strap two or three holes. Once in the saddle, adjust the length of your stirrups. When your leg is hanging straight down and the bottom of the stirrup iron touches the middle of your ankle bone, then the stirrup is the correct length. Make your horse stand quietly while you are mounting and adjusting your reins and stirrups.

To mount easily and correctly takes practice; once accomplished, you can mount any horse anywhere. No matter how gracefully you mount, you tend to pull the saddle crooked in the process, especially if the girth is not as tight as it should be. After you have confidence in mounting, you should use a mounting block, or convenient wall or get a "leg up." A leg up means that someone grasps your knee and ankle and throws you up on the horse. There is a danger in mounting this way. I have had very good friends throw me not only up but over the horse! So beware of practical jokers.

Now that you are "up," you will want to check your position on the horse to see if you are ready to walk. You should be sitting in the center of the saddle with your back straight but your weight slightly forward. If you look between the horse's ears, your head will take the right position. Don't look down at the horse as this will make you lean forward and round your shoulders. Your arms should drop naturally from your shoulders and your hands naturally from your wrists. Bend your elbows slightly; there should be a straight line from the elbow through your hands to the bit. Hold your hands several inches apart and just above the withers. If you have only a snaffle rein, it will enter your hand either outside your little finger or between it and your ring finger, whichever you prefer, and the ends will fall over your forefinger. If you have two reins (pelham or double bridle), the snaffle rein should enter your hand outside the little finger and the curb rein between the little finger and the ring finger. The ends of the reins should fall inside the reins on the right side.

The thumb is kept on the reins as they fall over the forefinger. This prevents the reins from slipping and keeps their ends in place. At first the two reins will seem like ten, and you may complain that you cannot handle them. But in a few rides you will wonder what you were ever grumbling about.

Your thigh, knee and calf should be firmly against the saddle with the lower leg falling back slightly from the knee. Push forward and down with your knees and then down into your heels with the balls of your feet on the inside of the stirrup irons and your feet approaching the parallel with your horse's body. If your toes turn out too much, they will pull your knee from the saddle; if they turn in too much they will cramp your whole leg.

This is the position that you will maintain while riding. As the horse's speed increases, your body will incline progressively

forward. Your lower leg will move when it is necessary to give the horse certain signals. Under most circumstances, this basic position will serve you well.

How do you know whether or not your position is correct? A mirror is revealing, but most of us do not have access to one as they are only found in large indoor rings. But there are many other ways of checking yourself. For example: as the horse moves out, if you fall backward or forward, if your hands jump up or your legs move, then something is wrong. If you look down at your knee and see your toe, if you feel uncomfortable, if you tire or stiffen quickly, then check your position.

But remember, it takes some time to be able to maintain the correct seat, even at a walk. Of course you will slide around and feel unsure at first. You will have to develop balance, relaxation and grip, all of which come by practice and from confidence in yourself and in the horse. Riding is a sport in which both the rider and the ridden are athletes, each learning his own particular job and how to work together.

To dismount: take the reins in your left hand with a short enough hold to prevent the horse from moving forward. Take your right foot from the stirrup. Pull up your right stirrup on the inside of the stirrup leather. Put your left hand on the horse's withers and your right hand on the pommel. Push your body up a little with your arms and swing your right leg over the horse's quarters. As your leg clears the quarters, bring your right hand to the center of the saddle to maintain balance. Drop your right leg alongside of your left, shifting all your weight to your arms, and slip your left foot out of the stirrup. Slide to the ground, pushing yourself slightly away from the horse. Don't throw yourself from the horse. Push your left stirrup up on the inside of its leather and take the reins over the horse's head. Dangling stirrups can get caught on things and annoy your horse.

Here are a few general principles to think about before you start your ride. A good rule to follow is "Walk the first half mile out and the last half mile in." Don't take off at a canter or even a trot the minute you get on the horse's back. Give him time to "warm up," to get his blood circulating, to loosen his muscles and open his windpipe, to adjust to the outside world after his stall. You wouldn't want to have to get out of bed and immediately run a mile in the heat or cold; then, don't ask your horse to do it. It will ruin his disposition as well as cause serious physical ailments. For the same reasons, don't work a horse right up to the barn door. Give him time to relax and cool out. Then you won't have the problem of your horse trying to jig or run toward home whenever you get within a mile of the stable.

If you must carry a whip, and don't unless you have to, carry the end of it between your thumb and forefinger in with the ends of your reins. Practice carrying it in either hand as when you need a whip you must be able to use it on whichever side is necessary. At first, do not try to use your whip with your hand on the reins. It is difficult not to jerk the horse's mouth in the process. Put the reins in one hand and use the whip on the flank —never around the head.

When you have been out a few minutes, check your girth. Put your leg in front of the saddle in order to grasp the billet straps. You will be able to regain your seat quickly if the horse makes a sudden move.

Beware of hard, rocky or boggy places while riding cross-country. Take them at a walk. Of course, out hunting you must sometimes gallop across them, but don't unless you must. The shock of pounding on a macadam road is bad for a horse's tendons and joints. The pull of a boggy place is not only hard on the tendons but often causes a lost shoe. The dangers of a rocky place are obvious.

If you are considerate of your horse you will be repaid with a sound, obedient mount. Remember, he is not a machine—you can't just step on the gas and go. And even machines run better with good care.

Holding the stirrup leather on the off side as the rider mounts in order to balance the saddle against her weight.

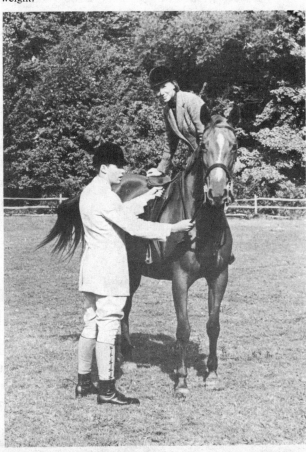

Chapter V

Sidesaddle

As the interest in riding sidesaddle is at a low ebb, we will not go into the art of riding this seat here. But rather let us take a quick look at the principles involved and the differences in the tack and habit. The seat certainly deserves better understanding and consideration than it is getting from the current generation. There is no more graceful sight than a lady sidesaddle on a mount with a good head carriage and way of going. Let us remember that all ladies rode sidesaddle until this century. They no more would be seen mounted astride than they would show their ankle or wear trousers!

A lady's attire when riding sidesaddle is called her habit and differs from that worn astride chiefly in the skirt which covers the britches. For formal wear the cloth should be dark blue or black and the headgear a bowler, or a silk hat with a heavy mesh veil fastened around the brim and covering the whole face. The saddle is substantially heavier due to its greater size and amount of padding. The panels are covered with linen which is cooler on the horse's back than leather. The leaping head provides a base of support for the right leg and the balance strap helps contradict the additional weight to the left by running from the right rear of the saddle, over the girth and buckling to the left billet. A third strap runs over the balance strap to hold down the right flap.

Those who argue for the sidesaddle seat praise its greater comfort for the rider on a long ride or hunt and its greater security for the ladies who lack the muscular strength and long legs of a man. But certainly the twentieth century woman with her increased participation in sports is more suited to riding astride than her grandmother. Those against the sidesaddle complain of the difficulty in fitting it to many horses and to a lessened "feel" of the horse by the rider. Although the rider is not likely to be bucked or jumped off a sidesaddle, she is more likely to be pinned under him if he falls. However, some old wives tales about the sidesaddle have been proven false; the balance strap does not make horses buck; the rider can be forward and with her horse over a fence, and she is not likely to develop curvature of the spine!

The objectives of the rider sidesaddle are the same as those of the rider astride; to direct the horse through his tasks with a balanced but firm seat in a controlled but relaxed manner. The rider sits as straight to the front as possible, shoulders square and level with the spine perpendicular to the horse's backbone. The right thigh lies along the top of the saddle and crosses the horse's backbone just behind the withers with the lower leg hanging straight down or slightly back. The left thigh is against the saddle at about a 45 degree angle and the

balance strap

lower leg is slightly back from the knee. The stirrup is adjusted in the same manner as astride with the ankle bone as a guide. To grip under ordinary circumstances the right thigh presses against the top of the pommel with the outside of the right lower leg pressed against the saddle and the left thigh and knee against the saddle. Under circumstances demanding a particularly strong grip as during a bucking session or an awkward jump the rider presses the left thigh forward and possibly up against the leaping head; the weight is consciously carried all along the right thigh and pressure with the outside of the lower leg is greatly increased. The rider carries her body erect but supple, and the hands are carried higher and further back than astride but still keeping a straight line from the elbow to the bit.

leaping head

cantle

strap holding down right flap

girth

balance strap

Chapter VI

Walking, Turning and Backing

Ready to walk? Then shorten your reins until you establish contact with the horse's mouth, that is, until you can feel his mouth lightly at the ends of the reins. If you have two reins, they should both be the same length. Establishing contact with the horse's mouth is your message to him that there is something you want him to do. When he feels the light pressure of the bit his head will come into position. If he is relaxed he will raise it; if he is gazing around admiring the scenery, he will straighten and lower his head. If he is resting one leg or standing sprawled out, squeeze with your legs without releasing the reins to bring his legs under him.

Collected walk.

By making contact with the horse's mouth, putting his head in the correct position and bringing his legs under him so that his weight is evenly distributed, you are collecting or gathering your horse and a collected horse is a balanced horse. Why is collection so important? When a horse is collected, his legs (motor), his head and neck (balancer), are in the best positions to carry out your commands. There are different degrees of collection. A horse performing a high school maneuver is highly collected while a horse at a normal, collected walk is less so. As you wish your horse to extend his gait, you abandon collection but you always keep your horse "in hand," that is, between your hands by contact and your legs by using them to keep him up to the bit. Without a rider a horse collects and balances himself naturally but the weight of the rider tends to destroy this balance. The horse wants to carry the added weight the easiest way which is to carry it all on the forehand. This makes him awkward and difficult to manage. Thus you must help him by collection or by keeping him in hand.

To move into a walk after collecting your horse, shift your weight slightly forward; squeeze with both legs; relax your hands releasing the reins as the horse lowers and stretches his head with the first step. With the use of these signals, a properly trained horse will walk out promptly and calmly. Unfortunately, not all horses are well trained. If the horse does not respond, more force must be used in the form of intermittent pressure with the calf or even kicking sharply just behind the girth. When using your legs, keep the inside muscles of your legs flat against the saddle. Don't let those knees turn out. At first this may be hard until your muscles stretch and flatten. As you practice, it becomes easier until you don't have to think about it at all.

As a horse walks, his head moves a little with each step. Your fingers will move a little in an opening and closing motion to keep a steady contact with his mouth. The key to soft contact is relaxation. When your hands and arms are stiff and do not

Alert, extended walk on a loose rein.

follow the motion of the horse's head, your horse will tell you by tossing his head or leaning on the bit. When you relax and your seat is secure, that is, when your weight is pushed down through your legs to your heels and your legs firmly against the saddle, your hands will improve. You will not tend to lean on the reins to keep your balance. So while you are walking around, check your position.

To turn let's say, to the right, shift your weight a little to the right, move your right hand slightly to the rear, close your fingers on the reins and "fix" your hand. This is called a direct rein. In other words, the hand which has been following the movement of the horse's head will now resist that movement. Don't pull the horse's head around; that isn't necessary. His head should be facing in the direction in which he is moving. If you are walking in a large circle, his head will turn only a little; if you are making a sharp turn, shorten your reins, increasing the

pressure so that his head will turn sharply. But don't pull out and down toward your knee with your hand. Your left hand will softly follow the movement of the horse's head, taking care not to contradict the instructions of the right hand, but ready to keep the head from turning too far. Your legs will remain still but ready to urge the horse forward if his pace slackens.

If your horse just turns his head but continues to walk in a straight line, squeeze him with your right leg to push his hindquarters slightly to the left, bending him around your leg so that he must turn. Your left leg will be ready to keep his hindquarters from moving too far to the left. When a horse feels the pressure of the legs, he wants to move away from it. So when you squeeze with both legs, he moves forward. When you squeeze with one leg, he moves to the side away from it.

If your horse strongly resists turning at all, carry your right hand to the right and close your fingers on the reins. This is called an opening or leading rein. Carry your left hand in front of the withers, not across them, pressing the rein against his neck. This is called a bearing rein. Use your legs to force the hindquarters to follow the circle.

When you are making a turn, imagine a drawing of the circle with the horse's legs moving on either side of the line. Then you won't make some of the common mistakes such as turning the horse's head too far to the inside or the outside of the circle, or swinging the hindquarters to the outside of the circle.

When using an indirect rein the hand is carried away from the straight line to the bit towards the center line of the horse. An indirect rein may be used in front of the withers or behind the withers. It is a more advanced aid and you will use it when asking certain precise movements of your horse.

To back: shorten your reins until you establish a firm contact with the horse's mouth. Shift your weight slightly backward; move your hands slightly to the rear closing your fingers on the reins; squeeze with both legs until your horse gives in to the pressure of the bit by taking a step back. As the step is completed, relax your fingers and legs to reward the horse. Repeat the movement until the horse has taken three or four steps. Be ready to use one leg more strongly than the other if the horse backs crookedly. After backing, always walk your horse forward a couple of steps as a reward and so that he can regain his normal balance.

One of the common faults in backing is that people forget to use their legs; they just pull. If you use only your hands, your

horse will overflex, that is, bring his chin in toward his chest, or raise his head rather than moving to avoid the pressure of the bit. If you use your legs, he will want to move. As your closed fingers on the reins will not let him go forward, he will have to go backward. His head and neck will remain in a normal position and his jaw will relax. Squeezing both legs with constant pressure (not intermittent) at the girth has the same effect as punching a person in the abdomen. It tends to double the horse up, getting his hindquarters under him.

To stop: shift your weight slightly backward; squeeze with your legs to bring the horse's legs under him; close your fingers on the reins and fix your hands. The second your horse responds, relax your fingers to reward him. In other words, when you stop your horse you simply collect him and then fix your hands.

You may say your horse has a hard mouth and will not stop with a light pressure on his mouth. Well, some horses do have tough mouths but this is because they have been hardened by bad hands. Pulling won't soften his mouth: it makes him want to pull back. If you patiently school (train) him, using the correct aids, he will improve.

What are aids? They are exactly what we have been talking about throughout this chapter: hands, legs, weight and voice. Voice has been neglected not because it isn't important, but because it is used less often than the others. Nothing is more soothing to a frightened horse than a steady hand and a quiet voice. The voice can help your other aids. For instance, if you have trouble stopping your horse, you can repeat firmly, "Whoa!" But never let your voice take the place of other aids. For instance, do not cluck instead of using your legs to move forward. Anyway, you would feel rather silly if you sat clucking to a well-trained horse and he stood there wondering what all the noise was about while he waited for your signals.

When moving on a straight line, use one aid at a time and follow one right after the other. When driving a car, you don't turn on the ignition, step on the gas, shift gears and take your foot off the clutch all at the same time. Then don't confuse your horse by applying all the aids at once. But do strive to apply your aids smoothly so that eventually they do seem to blend one into the other. Of course, when you are turning you apply your hands, legs and weight at the same time.

When you want to move out into a trot, canter or the hand gallop, you will apply the aids the same way as you do to walk. You will turn and stop the same way at faster gaits as at the walk. However, the aids become more important as your speed increases.

It can be fun practicing your aids at a walk. Practice turning by walking in a figure eight making the circles smaller and smaller until you come to a standstill. When you can keep a steady contact with the horse's mouth on the flat, see how well you do going up and down hills. Be sure to check your position once in a while. Is your weight really sinking through your legs into your heels? Are your arms relaxed with your elbows slightly

Trotting in a figure eight. An excellent exercise for the horse and rider. Also helpful in settling a fresh or excited horse. The first rider changed to the right diagonal in the middle of the figure eight for her circle to the left. The other riders are still on left diagonal during their right hand circle.

Stand in your stirrups and balance your upper body by placing your hands in front of the withers when you ride up a hill that is at all steep. By doing this you lighten the load on the horse's hindquarters allowing them to push more effectively.

bent? Can you stand in the stirrups for a few strides without leaning on the horse's neck or flopping back in the saddle? If so, then let's trot.

Chapter VII

Trotting Leads to...

Practice posting while walking and it will be much easier when you start to trot. Move slightly forward and upward out of the saddle and sink back gently. Count one for up and two for down to get the rhythm of it. Don't bend your back or hunch your shoulders as you move forward. Don't cheat and lean on the reins or the withers to get out of the saddle. If your position is correct, that isn't necessary. Of course, it is easier to post while actually trotting because the thrust of the horse's hind leg pushes you out of the saddle.

After collecting your horse and asking him to trot by squeezing with your legs, shifting your weight slightly forward and releasing the reins, sit to the first few trotting sides. This gives you time to feel the rhythm. Then move forward and up. Don't work at it too hard and don't move any higher out of the saddle than necessary. Let the horse do the work.

You don't have to heave yourself out of the saddle; the thrust of the horse's hind leg pushes you out. Some horses move with short, high strides and will throw you further out of the saddle than horses with long, low strides. But let the horse determine that and you just do as little work as possible.

Think for a minute how the horse's legs are moving at a trot. His right front leg and left hind leg are moving up and down at the same time and his left front leg and right rear leg are moving up and down at the same time. These are called "diagonals" as you can draw a diagonal line between the legs that are working together. When you post, you are moving up and down with one of these diagonals; otherwise you would just be bouncing.

Left diagonal.

If you have trouble posting smoothly, check on the position of your legs. They may have shot out in front of the girth. They are not much good to you there as they cannot properly support the weight of your body. When you sink into the saddle, your seat will be back near the cantle and it will be hard to get forward and up again. If your legs slide too far back toward the horse's tail, they will probably make you fall too far forward and be out of balance with the horse's forward thrust.

Your hands will play tricks on you too when you first start to trot. They will want to go up and down with your body. This comes from your elbows being too stiff (not opening when your body moves up) or from using the reins to pull yourself out of the saddle. It may also be caused by your body not moving forward as well as up. At a trot your hands are still because the horse is not moving his head. A good way to learn how to keep your hands still is to put your forefingers on either side of the withers.

We have already seen that you are always on a diagonal at a trot; that is, if you are not bouncing. If you are working in a circle, you should be on the outside diagonal. If you are moving to the right, you should be out of the saddle when the horse's left foreleg is in the air; you should be in the saddle when his left foreleg is on the ground. You don't have to lean over and peer at the leg to find out what it is doing; you can find out by simply glancing at the shoulder. Eventually you won't even have to look at the shoulder; you will be able to feel when you are on the correct diagonal.

What difference does being on the correct diagonal make? Very little to you, perhaps, but quite a bit to the horse. When trotting in a circle, the horse's outside hind leg has more ground to cover than the inside leg. If you are on the outside diagonal, the inside hind leg has the work of pushing you out of the saddle and so you are helping to balance the work of the two legs.

Like people, horses are right- or left-handed. If you let him, your horse would trot on the diagonal (hand) he prefers all the time. This would mean that only one hind leg would develop the muscle used to push you out of the saddle. So even if you are riding out in the country, make sure you change diagonals once in a while. Then your horse will not become one-sided.

One of the best exercises for you and your horse at a trot is the figure eight. Start out with large circles, making them smaller and smaller just as you did at a walk. As the circles get smaller, you will want to collect your horse more. Strive to keep an even pace throughout. Don't forget to change diagonals as you change direction in the center. To change diagonals, sit in the saddle for one beat, just one.

Do you want to develop a firm, relaxed seat? Then practice your sitting trot or the "close seat" as western cow hands ride.

Don't groan. It is not a punishment on you or the horse when done properly. Put your horse into a slow trot, also called a dog trot. The horse's rate of speed at a dog trot is about six miles an hour compared to about eight miles an hour at a regular trot. If your horse trots too fast, of course you will bounce around. Keep your weight pushed down to your heels with your leg muscles firm but relaxed. Don't lift your heels, and, gripping too hard, pinch with your knees. When you do this, you are actually pushing yourself out of the saddle.

After you are able to dog trot with stirrups, try it without stirrups. Cross the stirrups in front of the saddle so that they do not bang your ankles. It shouldn't be any harder than with stirrups. You also can post without stirrups. It is not too difficult—try it.

Work hard to develop smooth, perfectly timed posting because it prepares you for jumping. You move forward and up out of the saddle as the horse leaves the ground for a jump the same way you do at a trot. If you learn to wait for the horse's thrust to push you out of the saddle at a trot, you will be on the way to knowing that certain moment when the horse's thrust tells you to leave the saddle for a jump. This is called timing and one of the secrets of jumping is timing.

A cavalletti is a series of rails arranged at regular intervals in order to lengthen or shorten a horse's strides. The rails or logs should be rigid so that the horse cannot easily kick them out of place (note the ready-made solution to this problem in the photograph) and should be substantial enough to make the horse look at them but not high enough to make him jump. Thin telephone poles are excellent for this purpose. All horses benefit from work at a trot over rails arranged approximately five feet apart as it encourages them to lower and extend their necks to a position which is ideal in approaching a jump. It is also a good test of the stability of the rider's seat, particularly the strength of his drive into his heels. The rider must make every effort not to interfere with the horse either through his hands or a loose seat. Approach the cavalletti at a steady trot with a loose rein; stand in the stirrups if you cannot post without interfering with the horse's balance. A cavalletti can be a great help in teaching a horse to jump quietly and in reclaiming older horses that rush their fences. A horse can be encouraged to make his take-off earlier or later by the placing of the last rail of the cavalletti before the obstacle.

Trotting over the rails

Chapter VIII

The Canter and Gallop

Cantering is more than an increase in speed over the trot. Actually, it is very little faster than a brisk trot. The difference between trotting and cantering lies in the change in the order in which the horse's legs move, causing you to sit in the saddle rather than post. It is not any harder to learn than the trot. In fact, most people find it easier because of the balance, grip and confidence they have learned at the walk and trot.

As we have seen, when a horse trots two legs, diagonal front and hind, move up and down at the same time causing a definite one, two motion. At a canter each leg moves independently. The one, two, three, four movements of the legs blend and cause a smoother motion. You don't post as there is no distinct motion with which to post; there is no definite thrust to push you out of the saddle. You just sit on top of the horse and enjoy the rocking chair motion.

You may say it isn't that easy, that you bounce around. Are you leaning forward a little because the horse has increased his speed? Perhaps you are leaning too far forward and are "ahead of the horse." Of course, when you first start you will bounce around a little. Practice will cure that if your legs are firmly against the saddle and your weight is pushed down through your legs to your heels. Cantering is the first real test of whether you are doing this properly. At a walk and trot you can get away with just cocking your ankle down with no weight really pushing it down. You may fool your teacher, your friends and even yourself, but everybody will know when you canter. Remember, pushing your heels down is not just somebody's idea of what looks nice on a horse. If your weight drives through your legs to your heels, you will stay on your horse safely with the least amount of effort. After all, it is not much fun riding if you cannot stay on the horse!

54

Another reason you may be having trouble with your cantering is that you are too stiff. If you place a stick on a rolling surface, it will slide around and even fall off, while if you do the same thing with something soft like a cloth, it will tend to stay in place and move with the motion. Don't be stiff like a stick; relax and sit down in the saddle. Remember, you are not moving up and down out of the saddle but rather backward and forward in the saddle.

To move your horse into a canter, collect him and lean forward slightly. You will shorten your reins more than you do

at a trot because the faster you are moving, the further forward your body will be. Therefore your reins must be shorter to keep steady contact with the horse's mouth. Also, the faster the horse is going, the greater amount of pressure must be put on the reins to stop him. If your hands are back in your lap, you will have trouble stopping even the most obedient horse.

You will want to collect your horse a little more for a canter than for a trot so that his hind legs will be in the best position to give the push necessary. Then, too, you want all his attention turned to you, not half of it on his friends behind him and the other half on the colts playing in the next field. You should move into a canter from a walk unless you have a special reason for doing otherwise. This is good training for you and your horse. Make up your mind in advance which lead you want to be on and then put your horse on it.

What is a lead? When a horse canters, one front leg reaches out further and hits the ground sooner than the other front leg. If it is the right front leg, then the horse is on the right lead;

Cantering on the left lead.

if it is the left front leg, he is on the left lead. The horse's weight shifts to the side of the lead he is on and, when he goes around a corner, he actually leans to that side. The faster he goes and the sharper the turn, the further he leans. Consequently, if the horse goes around turns on the wrong lead, he is seriously out of balance. If he is on the left lead and turning to the right, he is being pulled in the opposite direction to where his weight and legs want to go. There are two dangers to this situation. His legs may shoot out from under him or he may cross his forelegs in order to keep his balance and trip himself. If you are wondering how this could happen, try running in a circle to the right and at the same time leaning to the left and see how it feels.

Now you may ask: Why do I have to put a horse on a certain lead if I am cantering down a straight path? Because a horse is a creature of habit. He learns by repetition. He is also a rather flighty animal and forgets things if they are not repeated. If you use the proper aids only some of the time, your horse will soon think: "Sometimes I get a set of signals which tell me to break on the left hand or the right; sometimes I am allowed to decide the lead for myself. From now on I think I will make the decision all of the time." When a horse adopts this frame of mind, taking the correct lead is a problem.

There is a definite series of aids used to put a horse on a lead. Stick to them and you will not have any problems. To put your horse, let's say, on the right lead, turn him slightly to the left with his hindquarters a little to the right using a left indirect rein. Use your left leg strongly with a squeezing pressure as far behind the girth as necessary and your right leg intermittently which asks for a faster gait. If your horse is properly collected and alert, he will move out promptly on the right lead. The reason he takes the right lead rather than the left is because of the position in which you have put him. By turning him to the left, you have opened or freed his right shoulder while cramping his left. By using your left leg steadily, you have shifted his weight toward the right. He is in a position where he wants to lead with the right foreleg because it is the easiest thing to do.

When you are learning to canter, the important thing is to get cantering. If your horse trots a few strides before cantering, let him go as long as he breaks on the correct lead. However, make him canter as quickly as possible. If you let him trot half way around the ring before he breaks, he will be uncollected and you will be in no position to enjoy your canter. So bring him back to a walk and start again. If your horse trots before breaking, don't post. This only encourages him to keep trotting and it puts you in a bad position to take up the sitting canter. Once your seat is secure, that is, once you are not leaning on the reins to keep your balance and are not bouncing, take up the canter from a walk. If he trots, then bring him back to a walk and start again. If you are having trouble getting him to cooperate, then you are probably doing something wrong. Check your aids or ask someone what the problem is.

How do you know what lead you are on? Watch the shoulders. The shoulder that is coming forward first and furthest tells you the lead you are on. You can feel a lead more distinctly than a diagonal and in a short time you will be able to feel what lead you are on. After you have been cantering a while, try to *feel* what lead you are on first and then check. Soon you won't have to peek at all.

As you move into a canter, don't bend far forward and to the side on which you want your horse to take the lead. Some people think that this helps their horse to take the correct lead. Actually, it prevents him from doing so because it adds weight to the shoulder you want free. Be careful, too, when you are looking to see what lead you are on; you don't have to stick your nose down to his shoulder to find out.

Remember, your legs never change position, except to give signals, no matter what you are doing. However, they may cause you some trouble when you first start to canter. They may shoot out in front of the girth, "out on the dashboard" as it is called. This will be caused by your weight not being far enough forward or your legs not being firmly enough against the saddle. If your legs are out in front of you, your seat will slide to the back of the saddle. This is hard on the horse's loins and it is hard on you because the action of the hindquarters will bounce you around. If your weight is not driving your heels down, your legs will slide back toward the horse's tail. Then, your only way of staying on will be to grip as hard as you can with your knees which will not give you a very secure seat. Colonel John Barry, director of horsemanship at Fort Riley and captain of the Olympic Equestrian Team, told a story which shows the principle of grip. He said to take a watermelon seed between your thumb and forefinger. You hold it gently but firmly if you don't want to drop it. But you cannot press too hard with your fingers or it will pop out from between them. When you apply this to grip, you will see if you depend wholly on your knees

to stay on, you will be actually pinching the horse out from under you.

The horse above has just made a flying change of lead from the left to the right. A "flying" change is accomplished at the canter or gallop. Once a rider has advanced to the stage of cantering across the country, showing or foxhunting, he should at least understand and be able to encourage his horse to change leads when he changes direction. Most horses will do this naturally if given a chance.

An easy way to teach yourself and your horse to make a flying change is to canter in a figure eight, slow to a trot in the center, and then break off on the opposite lead. Keep decreasing the trotting strides until the horse is only taking one or two before breaking on the new lead. To make a flying change correctly he must be collected, balanced and calm.

To change from the left to the right lead: shift your weight to the left seatbone; use a left indirect rein and left leg just behind the girth (to free the right shoulder), and the right leg actively further behind the girth (to place the hindquarters so that the right hindleg alights on a line drawn between the forelegs). To cause this change in the horse's leg position the aids must be applied in sequence but almost simultaneously starting as the left hindleg pushes off and accomplishing the change of lead in the period of suspension that follows. To do this on demand the horse must receive clear instructions from a firm seat and distinct aids applied at the right moment. But even a relative beginner can collect his horse and shift his weight when approaching a sharp turn. A horse galloping around a bend on the wrong lead is a danger to himself and his rider.

Once in a while you will run into a horse that is difficult to get on a certain lead. He is very right- or left-handed. The patient application of the correct aids and the determination to make him break properly should correct the problem in time.

However, I hope you never run into a horse like the one a friend brought me once. "This horse absolutely will not break on the left lead," said he. "We will straighten that out for you in a few minutes," said I. To make a long story short, half an hour later the horse finally broke on the correct lead. Then it took another twenty minutes to get him to repeat the performance.

The moral of the story is: patience and more patience and . . .

The hand gallop is simply an extended and faster canter. As the horse moves faster into the hand gallop, you will feel uncomfortable in the saddle because you are behind the motion. You will also feel insecure as the increased drive of the hindquarters pushes you out of the saddle.

Then stand in the stirrups, leaning slightly forward to "catch up to the motion of the horse." By taking your weight out of the saddle you will not only be up with your horse but you will be freeing his motor (hindlegs) so that it can drive faster.

It is not hard to stay in this position. Your weight sinks into your knees and heels, and your ankles act as shock absorbers. The forward drive of the horse keeps you out of the saddle.

You will have shortened your reins because the horse has increased his speed. Your hands will move down and forward as the horse extends and lowers his head and neck with his extended stride. Although the horse has increased his speed, he will still be "in hand." You will be pushing him up to the bit with your legs and at the same time be steadying him with your hands. It is a wonderful feeling, this controlled surge of power as you move out across an open field.

The full gallop is an unrestrained hand gallop. Your horse moves faster. His head and neck extend further. His stride lengthens and flattens out. Your body moves further and further forward as the horse's speed increases. You lighten the pressure on the bit, allowing the horse to move faster, but you always keep contact with his mouth. If you "throw the reins away," you are asking your horse to run. And run away he will. He also might stumble or shy at something and you will be in no position to control or help him.

If you feel your horse is starting to run away with you, don't start pulling steadily on the reins; he will just lean on the bit and run faster. Use a series of half-halts to stop him. A half-halt is a firm, upward action on the reins followed quickly by a relaxing of the fingers and a releasing of the reins. You can use a series of half-halts with both hands or just one hand, and with varying degrees of severity as you think necessary. The time to stop a runaway is when you feel yourself *starting* to lose control—not after the horse is running full steam.

At a hand gallop and gallop be prepared. Watch out for holes and gullies. Collect and steady your horse on the turns. Don't gallop him on hard or rocky ground or on macadam roads, especially down hills. This is bad for his tendons. Of course, if you are out foxhunting or racing, some of these rules must be ignored in the interest of the sport. But in ordinary riding you will do well to keep them in mind. Your horse does not have to be taught how to gallop. Nature teaches him this because it is his greatest means of self-defense. He can out-run almost any other four-legged animal.

When you increase your speed do so quietly and slowly: canter, hand gallop, gallop. And remember, the faster he is going, the longer it is going to take him to stop. So stop him slowly and quietly. Of course, he must obey your signals promptly but allow him more space to stop from a gallop than, let us say, from a trot. If you stepped down hard on the gas

every time you started your car and slammed on the brakes
every time you wanted to stop it, it would wear out quickly.
Horses wear out too.

Chapter IX

Understanding Your Horse...

Now that you can walk, trot, canter and gallop, you will be riding your horse more cross-country. How surprised you will be by the change in him when you get away from the ring or field. He will perk up and do all sorts of things that he would never do on home ground. You may get your first fall when riding cross-country. Don't be afraid of it or any fall. If you do any amount of riding, it is bound to happen. You may have many falls but you do not have to be hurt, not even slightly. Just remember: if you feel yourself falling, relax and don't throw your hands out. Try and curl yourself into a ball and when you land on the ground, roll away from the horse. Don't try to keep hold of the reins. It will not stop you from falling and you may pull the horse on top of you or pull yourself under the horse. Falls are to be avoided but not worried about. The most experienced riders have them. Just this winter I was ignominiously dumped in the middle of a stream. It had been a long

day out hunting and I was thinking of a warm fire rather than my riding. We walked down a bank and my horse reached quickly for a drink, catching me off balance. I gracefully somersaulted into a foot and a half of icy water. Even the horse thought it was funny.

If you make a real attempt to understand your horse, you will know why he gives a little buck on a crisp morning or shies at a white stone which he has passed a dozen times before without even deigning to notice it. Understanding your horse is just as much a part of good horsemanship as good form. The better you understand your horse, the more fun you are going to have. The first step in getting to know your horse is to practice putting yourself in his shoes. Pretend you are a horse that has just been taken from a cozy stall and had his warm blanket pulled off. It is a cold morning and to add insult to injury, he gets a cold saddle slapped on his back. So he tries to nip the nearest thing to him which is usually you. Of course you will slap him across the muzzle for being bad. But if you think a moment, you won't slap him too hard because you really don't blame him. And the next time you will be a bit more gentle.

When a horse is bad you must always punish him; when he is good you must always reward him. This is the only way he can learn. This does not mean you must always hit him with a crop or give him a piece of sugar. There are many ways

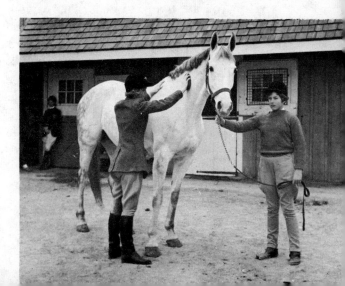

of punishing or rewarding him. A pat on the shoulder or a carrot are some rewards. A good grooming for a good day's work is even better. We have already seen some of the ways to reward your horse while riding: letting him walk freely when he has successfully completed an exercise; easing the pressure on the bit the second he responds to it; keeping your weight up with his movement and not back on his loins.

There are many ways of punishing your horse. Use a crop on his flanks or use your legs strongly if he has been particularly bad. Like rewards, there are many little punishments you may give him as you ride along: make him repeat a movement until he does it correctly (he gets just as bored as you do); increase the pressure on the bit when he doesn't respond. Your ruling principle in reward and punishment is: "Be consistent." Don't punish him for something once and ignore it the next time. Always make the punishment fit the crime. You only can do this if you understand why he committed the crime in the first place. If you are not sure, it is better to be wrong by punishing him too lightly than too much.

Your rewards and punishments must be given immediately. Your horse learns principally from memory. Therefore it must be made clear to him what is right and what is wrong. Your horse is flighty. He finds it much easier to forget things than to learn them. But if you practice good riding habits, your horse will develop good working habits.

When you are trying to understand your horse, remember that he thinks of only one thing at a time. If a fly bites him, he will kick out at it even if you are in the range of his kick. He will not think that he is going to hurt you but simply that he is going to get rid of that fly. So whenever you walk behind a horse, and don't unless you must, or work around his hind legs, pat him on the hindquarters and talk to him. This will let him know you are there and will keep his attention turned to you.

Are horses stupid? Many people say they are but I don't agree. Horses do some stupid things. They will eat and drink so much that they will make themselves sick. But surely horses running free didn't do this. Man has domesticated the horse and in doing so has destroyed some of the horse's natural instincts and put the horse in environments that are not natural to him. If we do not compensate for what we have taken away from the horse then he will do stupid things. We all have known some very clever horses. We have also seen some supposedly stupid horses do some very clever things. Without becoming too deeply involved in an age-old argument, I will simply say that the horse is smart enough to take good care of himself. When you are riding and get into a tight situation, leave him alone and while he is taking care of himself he will take care of you.

A horse is a more nervous animal than a cat or dog. If you raise your arm suddenly, it will seldom startle a house pet but will almost always startle a horse. Because a horse's eyes are set on the side of his head he can see much further to the side than we can, but he cannot see clearly. Keep this in mind when you are moving around him.

If your horse could live in the house with you, he would not be so nervous. Notice how much more relaxed is the horse that has had a lot of gentle handling than the horse that has been neglected or ill-treated. A thoroughbred or near thoroughbred is more nervous by nature than a half-bred or cold-blooded horse due to his finer breeding. But the temperament of a horse is determined chiefly by the manner in which he is raised and how he is treated from day to day. So always be quiet and patient and never lose your temper with your horse.

If you keep in mind this nervous and rather timid nature of the horse, you will not approach him suddenly, throw or wave equipment near him or do any one of a dozen things which are apt to frighten him. If you are patient with your horse you will have a quiet horse in return. When you are out riding you will be understanding when he shys at a rabbit or a piece of paper; he may be momentarily frightened. With regard to shying, more allowance should be made for a "green" or inexperienced horse than for an older horse. Make the green horse walk quietly up to the object; talk to him and pat him on the shoulder to reassure him. If you punish him for shying when he is really frightened, he will associate punishment with a bad experience and be more frightened the next time. However, when an older horse shys, it is usually caused by high spirits. If so, punish him with your legs and make him walk smartly up to the object. But you must first determine whether it is playfulness or fear which has made him shy.

Basically a horse is not a particularly affectionate animal. He does not get the benefit of your constant companionship. But he is not without any affection at all. Be quiet and kind while working with your horse and while riding him. Visit him once in a while and talk to him; give him an apple or a handful of oats. A good grooming is one of the things a horse likes best, better than all the petting you could give to him. Feed and water him regularly, keep him clean and love him and he will love you.

Trust your horse but don't ask him to do things that he is unable to do either from lack of ability or training. Ride confidently, "throwing your heart ahead of you." Be consistent in your commands and in your rewards and punishments, and you will have a trustworthy and confident mount.

Chapter X

Helps You With Your First Jumps...

The speed with which a fence is taken makes it difficult to analyze precisely the actions of a rider and a horse over a jump. Study the pictures of jumping that follow. Then while you watch your friends schooling or in the show ring, look for what you see in the pictures. Understand what the horse actually does with himself over a jump and how the rider adapts himself to the horse's efforts. Then you know what you must learn.

When jumping, the horse's head and neck move in coordination with his legs, helping him maintain his balance. As he approaches a fence, he lowers his head, measuring the height and distance of the obstacle and adjusting his stride for the take-off. Ideally, his stride lengthens as he nears the fence. However, sometimes the horse or rider makes a mistake in judgment; the horse must then shorten his last few strides or put in a quick one to be in a good position to take off.

His neck flexes as his front legs leave the ground and his hind legs push off. Over the jump his head and neck stretch out as his front legs start to reach for the landing. On landing, his head raises but his neck extends even further. As his hind legs land his front legs start the new stride, his head and neck regain their normal position for the canter.

70

The higher the jump the more pronounced these actions are. If his legs do not move far off the ground, then his head and neck only change their position slightly. You will notice that his front legs land in a one-two order. If he landed on both front legs at the same time it would cause quite a jolt, not only for you but for the horse's tendons. Some horses do jump this way but they are bad jumpers.

Horses jumping without a rider, in a corral or on a longe rope, are remarkably graceful. They seldom make a mistake. Moral: when a horse makes a mistake at a fence it is usually the rider who caused it. As Rigan McKinney, the great steeplechase rider, said: "Have you ever seen a loose horse fall?"

Jumping is one of the most exciting experiences of riding. You feel a sense of challenge approaching a fence, exhilaration clearing it and satisfaction as you canter on to the next one. Of course you want to jump as soon as possible. But don't start too soon and run the risk of a bad experience. Wait until the person who is helping you learn the sport says you are ready. And wait until you are *sure* you want to jump. Don't spoil your fun by starting while you still have reservations about it or while your seat is insecure.

Naturally you will be a bit uncertain at first. You are doing something you have never tried before and everyone is a little afraid of the unknown. Confidence is the keynote to success. Have confidence in yourself, your instructor and your horse and any fears will quickly disappear.

To gain this confidence you can practice jumping without actually going over a fence. Place a rail on the ground and take up the trot. The horse will not jump it but you will learn the jumping position. About four or five strides from the "fence," take the position of the hand gallop or posting trot out of the saddle. That is, take up a two-point contact, knee and calf, as against the three-point contact, seat, knee and calf, of the walk, sitting trot and canter. This will be your position for learning to jump.

At the same time you take this position, place your hands about a third of the way up the horse's neck and grasp the mane or, if he has no mane, a stirrup strap buckled around the horse's neck. Hold this position over the rail and then resume the posting trot. Repeat this exercise until you automatically take your position and place your hands on the horse's neck. Practice approaching the rail absolutely straight and at an even pace. The horse should neither speed up nor slow down as he makes his approach.

When you feel confident at a trot, take up a slow canter. It is more likely that your horse will make a little hop over the rail while he is cantering. But, whether he "jumps" or not, you will be in the correct position.

So you want to jump. Then make sure that you are on a quiet, safe jumper and go to it. If you have your own horse and don't know how he jumps, or you know he is unreliable, then borrow a horse to learn on. You should be able to pay most of your attention to what you are doing and as little as possible to such problems as refusing, ducking out or running away. Jump fences with wings while you are learning. You are just a passenger over your first fences and the wings help guarantee that your horse will take you down the right track.

Adjust a rail just high enough off the ground to make your horse jump; eight inches to a foot ought to do it. Start out jumping it from a trot. Don't grab the mane until you get to the edge of the wings. You want to keep contact with the horse's mouth as long as possible so that you can keep him under control.

As you go over the fence, make sure the weight of your upper body is resting on the horse's neck and that you are not staying on by holding the mane and leaning back. Take hold of the mane only to be prepared for emergencies. No matter what you or the horse does you cannot jerk him in the mouth if you have a fistful of the mane. It will also help you keep your balance if either of you makes a mistake.

The next thing to check is that your weight is down in your heels. Your head should be up, your eyes looking between the horse's ears. Be careful to stay out of the saddle until the horse has landed on the far side of the fence and has started his first stride. You may have a strong tendency to come back into the saddle too soon. Most beginners do. Once you can hold your position at a trot, start jumping from a canter.

As you jump, concentrate on when the horse takes off. This is something you partly see and partly feel. With practice you should be able to tell where his last three strides are going to place him. For instance: if he is cantering freely and the end of one stride is at the edge of the wings then you can see that he will probably take only one more stride before the take-off. Ponies will probably take two. If the horse is at a trot or a collected canter he will probably take two strides (three for a pony) in the wings. Principally you *feel* when the horse takes off. You will *feel* him measuring his fence and you will *feel* the push of his hind legs as he leaves the ground. As you are out of the saddle and have hold of the mane at this stage of your jumping, you do not have to move when the horse takes off. However, when you go on to more advanced jumping, timing the take-off will be essential to a good jump. So start thinking about it now.

When you are confident over low fences you will be ready for the next step in your progress toward your goal in jumping: to be with your horse. So far you have just been along for the ride. As you approach the fence, don't move your hands to the horse's neck until he leaves the ground. You will now have control of the horse until the last second. You also must time the take-off to a certain degree. By now you should stop grabbing the mane. Put your hands on the horse's neck. If you or the horse makes a mistake and you feel it necessary, you can take hold of the mane in a split second. The rider, shown on the opposite page, was "left behind" but avoid hurting the pony's mouth by keeping his hands forward and relaxed.

Jump! Jump! Jump! That is the way to learn. But be con-

"Left behind."

siderate of your horse or pony. Too much jumping or jumping the same fence continually will sour the most willing animal. Try to have several fences to practice over. Different kinds of jumps such as wall, brush, chicken coop, picket, will also be more fun for you. Set up a series of in and outs, that is, fences set one after the other where the horse can take only one or two strides between. This is a good test for your horse as well as for you. It makes him handy (clever) and will slow him down if he has a tendency to rush his fences.

You can raise the height of your jumps now. Practice jumping at different speeds, up hill and down, in the ring and across country. Above all, have fun.

If you run into some problems, don't hesitate to return to lower fences at slower speeds. You will progress faster if you retrace your steps a bit when you run into trouble rather than plunging on, hoping that the problems will correct themselves. You may also avoid a nasty fall.

Practice jumping low fences up and down hill to improve the security of your seat and your control of the horse. Above: to jump uphill increase the drive of the horse's hindquarters with your legs as he must jump several inches higher than the actual height of the fence. Below: to jump downhill keep your horse collected and jump from a trot when possible. The horse pictured took only one cantering stride before jumping.

Chapter XI

And in Advanced Jumping.

Do the fences that just a short time ago looked tremendous, seem smaller now? Has it been a long time since you were left behind or came back in the saddle too soon? Are your legs staying firmly in place because your weight is down in your heels? If you can answer yes to these questions, then you are ready for more advanced jumping.

Excellent bareback position.

To be more with your horse, maintain a three-point contact, cantering position, until the horse takes off. Until now you have taken up a two-point contact, hand-gallop position, several strides from the fence, avoiding any chance of being left behind. However, there are important advantages to approaching a fence with the three-point contact. Your seat is more secure; you have more control of your horse as your hands and legs are in a better position to act; you have a greater feeling of your horse.

Approach the fence with a three-point contact, your upper

body as far forward as the horse's speed demands. *Wait* for the thrust of the horse's hind legs on take-off to push you out of the saddle. Remain out of the saddle until the horse lands and starts a new stride. You will be "left" a few times but this does not necessarily have to be punishing to the horse. You will move your hands forward and perhaps grab the mane so that you will not jerk his mouth. You can still move out of the saddle even after take-off. If you are badly left you can let the reins slip through your fingers as the horse extends his neck.

Wait until the horse throws you out of the saddle on take-off. Don't anticipate him by moving too soon. If you do so you will not really be with the motion and you will upset his balance. When you move your hands to the horse's crest, check that the

reins are loose enough to allow for the full extension of his head and neck. Be careful not to flop back into the saddle after the jump; sink back gently. If you find yourself bobbing, that is, bending too low with your face in the horse's mane, you can correct it quickly by keeping your eyes up.

The last step toward jumping with your horse is to maintain a steady, light contact with his mouth over the fence. Instead of your hands moving to the horse's neck on take-off, they will now follow the movement of the horse's head, keeping the same light pressure throughout. To do this your seat must be secure. You must have full confidence in your horse. Your reins must be short enough during the approach to have a nice feel

of the horse's mouth. Over the fence the horse's head will carry your hands forward and downward; you do not move them independently. Throughout the movement you will keep a straight line between your elbow and the horse's mouth. If you lift or lower your hands you will interfere with his mouth and therefore his jumping.

One of the greatest dangers to avoid when jumping and keeping contact with the horse's mouth is the hands moving up on take-off or landing. If you are caught late or you are not

up with your horse, then you must move your hands forward. If you secretly don't want to jump a fence and are subconsciously hanging back, it will show up in your hands. This is why we say to throw your heart over the fence first. If your ankles are not doing their job as shock absorbers, then your hands will tend to jump up on landing. And, of course, if you come back into the saddle too soon the same thing will happen.

To be completely with your horse over a fence takes long practice. The fluid movement of body and hands will not come all at once. Don't be discouraged. Even good riders must grab a piece of mane once in a while. Anyone can jump well. All it takes is work.

Some horses tend to weave or wander during the approach to a fence. Others tend to jump at an angle. Schooling over lower obstacles and the use of guide rails as shown will help.

A bold, free jump by the horse over a three foot three inch gate. A timid horse will become more confident if he is only asked to jump new obstacles when they are low i.e. under three foot.

The horse is jumping a three foot, nine fence without strain. Note the rail a few inches off the ground and placed twenty-four feet in front of the principal obstacle. This is helpful in forcing a horse to slow down his approach and drop his head. It also places the horse for a good take-off without putting on him the demands of a full-sized in and out.

A horse that habitually takes off too late can be forced to take off sooner by a rail placed in front of the jump. Note that although the rider lost some of his drive into his heels he has kept in balance with the horse's movement and allowed the horse enough rein to stretch his head and neck. The fence is three feet, six inches high.

Chapter XII

The Care of Your Horse...

My own horse! What wonderful words they are! It is a great privilege to have your own horse, and a great responsibility. Man has tamed horses and taught them to serve him. In doing so he has made them dependent on him for food and care. If a horse is shut in a stall without food or water, or is turned out in a sparse pasture with a stagnant pond, he is helpless. If you want your own horse, you must recognize his dependence on you and be willing to give him proper housing and care.

Proper housing consists in furnishing a box stall or a standing stall. A box stall is the more desirable as it provides adequate room for him to move around as well as lie down. A horse cannot move freely in a standing stall; he must be tied with a rope. This rope must be long enough for him to reach his hay and water but short enough so that he cannot get a leg over it. Whether it be a box stall or a standing stall, a horse's shelter requires plenty of light, good ventilation and a floor of clay.

Horses are born with the instinct to be free. If at all possible, your horse should be able to look at the outside world. If he is shut in a dark, enclosed place, he will not only be unhappy, but he will develop bad habits such as stall walking and cribbing.

A horse needs not only a stall to protect him from the weather, but also a pasture of approximately one acre of good grass. A water supply in the pasture is essential. A stream is best as a trough is difficult to keep clean. Pasture does not merely provide grass for your horse: it is his playground and exercise area as well.

A horse needs oats and hay for feed. The oats should be clean, plump and heavy. Timothy is the basic hay. Mixed with some clover and orchard grass, it will provide a well-balanced diet for your horse. Alfafa is good for your horse and should be fed regularly in small quantities so that your horse's system can adjust to it. Alfafa acts as a laxative and in unregulated quantities can scour a horse. As there are many different kinds of hay and combinations of hay, it is best to get an experienced person's advice when buying it. The most important quality to look for in hay is that it is clean—free from dust and mold.

You can use different kinds of bedding such as peat moss and corn stalks but the most satisfactory type is good straw. A horse can get heaves and colic from bad straw as well as bad hay. Do not scrimp on the amount you use. A good thick bed will not only insure the comfort of your horse, but it will guard against thrush. Stalls need a thorough cleaning once a day.

How much do you feed your horse? Every horse is different, and how much as well as what to feed him is something you must work out yourself. The chart will give you a general idea. Keep in mind that a horse's stomach is quite small in relation to his size and that he has poor eating habits. Given the opportunity, he will eat until he is sick. So you must think for him where it concerns his stomach. Feed him in small quantities as often as possible. It is better to give him three feeds of three quarts each than two feeds of four-and-a-half quarts each. If your horse is working hard and requires large quantities of oats, try to give them to him in four feeds.

FIRST AID KIT

Colic medicine
Alcohol
Iodine
Bluing
Absorbine
Vaseline

Epsom salts
Body wash
Witch hazel
Lanolin
Cotton
Bandages

FEEDING CHART

	Worked every day divided in 3 feeds	Turned out divided in 2 feeds	Not worked; standing in stall divided in 2 feeds
Thoroughbred horse	10-12 quarts	8-10 quarts	½ normal feed
Halfbred horse	8-10 quarts	6-8 quarts	½ normal feed
Large pony	4-6 quarts	2-4 quarts	½ normal feed
Small pony	2-4 quarts	2 quarts	½ normal feed

Feed in this order: water, hay, oats. If your horse always has water in front of him, then you can give him his grain without worrying about his drinking a quantity after his meal. Make sure his water is clean and that in the winter it is not icy. Never permit your horse to gulp a whole bucket or more after being worked or fed.

Summer Care

In addition to the cleaning equipment mentioned earlier, you will need a scraper for the summer. When your horse breaks out in a sweat it will take a long time to cool him out if you don't give him a bath. To a bucket of warm water add a few drops of body wash to kill bacteria or absorbine to aid muscle tone. Use plenty of water: your horse enjoys it. Wash his mane and tail often to keep them free of ticks. Scrape him thoroughly but gently but do not scrape his legs as you would irritate the bones. Then take a towel and rub his head and legs being careful to dry the pasterns and heels.

A bath does not take the place of cooling out your horse. If you wash a horse that is hot not only from the weather but from work, you run the risk of foundering him or of giving him a chill. Walk your horse after his bath until he is absolutely dry except perhaps for his legs. Don't take too long with the bath: wash, scrape, rub and get moving.

Some horses do well on pasture, others do not. Some horses can stay out day and night, be ridden daily and, if the grass is plentiful, have no need for hay and oats. Others need a feed when they have been ridden. The flies bother some horses so that they have to be kept in during the day but can be turned out at night. Other horses, usually thoroughbreds, cannot be turned out at all during the summer because the flies have a feast on their tender skin. The climate, the flies, the condition of the pasture—all these things must be taken into consideration when you decide how to summer your horse. His condition will tell you how good your judgment is.

Winter Care

If you are going to do much riding during the winter you will have to clip your horse. For foxhunting he will need a full clip. Otherwise a "hunting clip" (only the neck, sides and flanks clipped) will be sufficient. This will leave him with some coat on his back to keep him warm. If your horse is not clipped and your stable is not drafty, a blanket is unnecessary. With a hunting clip he will need one blanket; with a full clip he will need a heavy sheet and a blanket.

A horse needs more feed in the winter than in the summer. A good feed will help to keep him warm. You can replace a couple of quarts of oats with corn. Give him lots of good hay and increase his grain. He should be "mashed" once a week if he is not working and twice a week if he is. Give him a mash after foxhunting. To make a mash mix equal parts of bran and oats; add some blackstrap molasses, salt and a handful of linseed or flaxseed. Mix with boiling water until wet through but not sloppy. Cover and let sit about an hour, stirring a few times so that the bottom is cooled too. Feed while warm.

If the weather is bad and your horse isn't worked or turned out, cut the grain considerably and make one of his meals a mash. Of course he can have all the hay he wants. Good quality hay is a sound investment because you do not have to feed so much grain. Grain is an energy food. A horse must be worked hard enough to use up the energy you feed into him. If he is not, rest assured, he will invent work for you!

General Care

A horse receives a tetanus toxide shot once in his life and a booster shot once a year afterward. He can get a tetanus infection from a simple scratch from a wire fence, so it is important that he have his yearly booster to combat this danger. However, if your horse gets a deep cut, see that he receives a booster immediately even if he had one a couple of months before. A horse is wormed twice a year. As there are many different kinds of worms, take a specimen to the veterinarian so that your horse can be wormed for the particular kinds he has. Have his teeth checked twice a year. They develop sharp points which make it difficult for him to eat and make the bit bothersome. These points must be floated (filed down). This is of particular importance in a young horse.

A horse's feet grow quickly and must be checked *at least* every six weeks. If he has shoes on, they should be reset, that is, the shoes removed, the feet dressed (trimmed and shaped) and the shoes reset. Your horseshoer will tell you when new shoes are needed. In the winter the horse must be shod for the icy and frozen going. Borium, drops of hard steel added to the shoes, is probably the best solution. If your horse is unshod, his feet should be dressed.

All your horse's equipment should fit properly and be kept clean. Blankets and sheets should be aired regularly. If you wipe the bit and the underneath of the saddle and the inside of the girth soon after you have taken them off, you will save yourself work later. Wash your leather with a damp cloth or sponge before applying saddle soap. You are just kidding yourself if you put the soap on top of the dirt. Wring your sponge out well before applying the soap. Water will dry out the leather. Rub the soap into the leather well, paying particular attention to the places where steel rests on the leather: buckles, bit and stirrups.

Common sicknesses like colic, azoturia and founder can be avoided by regular and sensible exercise and feeding. Thrush, scratches, shoe boils, coughs and colds can be avoided by good care. If your horse does get sick, or if he gets a bad bump or cut, or develops a lameness, call your vet immediately. You may lose your horse by not calling your vet.

Lungeing

If you own your horse, someday you will find it necessary or advisable to lunge him. A sore back or bad weather may prohibit riding but a ring of manure can provide decent footing in ice or snow. Or perhaps your horse is young and the easy way for him to get rid of his bucks is on a lunge rope. Lungeing is almost essential in breaking a colt. It teaches him cooperation and quietness while building muscle and coordi-

The cavesson, lunge rope and whip.

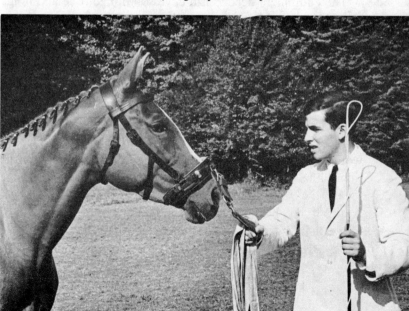

Working on about two-thirds of the lunge line at a collected trot.

nation without the strain on young bones and tendons of carrying weight. The lunge can be a great aid in schooling a green horse or improving an older one over fences.

The equipment needed is a cavesson, lunge rope and lunging whip. An older horse that is quiet and experienced may safely be worked on just a halter with a hunting whip available to urge him on if he becomes too sluggish. The cavesson is much like a halter with a ring in the center of the padded noseband. A throatlash and jowl strap keep the cheekpieces from sliding towards the horse's eyes, and it is important that the equipment be snugly fitted. A loose noseband, although padded, could cause injury to the delicate nose area and would inflict more punishment than intended by tugs on the lunge line. The lunge line is made of a tape-like material to lessen the risk of burning the horse's legs or the trainer's hands if the horse becomes rambunctious. Never wrap the lunge tightly around your hand as you may be unable to release it if the horse bolts. The lungeing whip (see illustration) consists of a firm, fibrous material approximately five feet in length, with an attached lash of approximately six feet.

If your horse does not lunge properly, start from the beginning as you would with a colt. Be patient and quiet and in a few days he should work well at a walk and trot. Remember that you are teaching him many things aside from moving in a circle, such as obedience to voice and gesture, balance, agility and calmness.

The ideal area is partially or totally enclosed in order to help guide the horse in the circle. Lead the horse in this circle, stopping frequently with a gentle pressure on the line and a firm "whoa"; then gradually drop further back and urge him to walk in a slightly larger circle. If the horse will walk in a big enough circle to use half the line, you are doing very well for the first day. Use the whip quietly to enforce your commands as he walks away from you; point it in front of his nose as you say "whoa", at his shoulder to encourage him to move away from you, from behind up towards his croup with the commands to walk, trot and canter which you can re-enforce with clucking sounds. Before you start actual lessons,

Assistant encouraging filly to use the full
length of the lunge line and to extend her trot.

the horse should be acquainted with the whip and have no fear of it.

As the horse shows a willingness to use all of the line you may need an assistant for a couple of days in order to help you keep up forward motion (see illustration). You should have little trouble if you keep the lungeing hand in a leading position and the whip pointed towards his hindquarters, and do not ask for a faster speed until you have full control and cooperation. If the horse has been frightened and proves to be balky, a mounted assistant leading the horse from the far side for a few days should solve the problem. Be sure to work the horse an equal amount of time in each direction and make him stop with his head in the direction he is moving; then walk up to his head and turn him around to change direction. Flip the lunge up and down if he starts to buck and give it gentle tugs to slow or stop him. You have considerable leverage on the horse's nose so pull on the line with discretion. A young or badly balanced horse may have trouble cantering in a small circle so do not ask the impossible but rather keep at a trot for several days more and then ask for only half a circle at the canter.

Do not attempt to lunge your horse over fences until he is working perfectly on the flat. And no matter how well he is performing you should have a helper available during the first lessons. The fence should have no obstacle such as a high standard (post) on the trainer's side that might catch the lunge line. Two wings lined up "head to tail" on the far side of the fence will help guide the horse. Lead and then lunge the horse over the rail on the ground so that he will know what is expected of him. Then urge him to trot over a low rail several times before asking him to canter over a fence of any size. At all times the trainer must allow the horse to approach the jump and move on afterwards in as straight a line as possible. Lungeing will build the horse's confidence and teach him to jump without excitement. It will also aid him in learning how to use himself over an obstacle without the distracting weight of the rider.

Vanning

In this motorized world it is essential for most people that their horses load and ride quietly in a trailer or van. Once a horse becomes frightened over the procedure, you will have a hard job restoring his confidence. Always allow more than enough time to load and drive to your destination as the horse will sense the excitement if you are in a hurry. Treat the horse as you would a colt if you know that he has never been vanned or has problems in this area. Practice loading the horse several times, taking all the time necessary and making much of him with soothing words, petting and feeding.

To load a horse on a trailer the person leading should have a good handful of hay or other feed to tempt the horse forward, distract him if he becomes excited and encourage him

Loading on a trailer. The person leading is offering the horse some hay while the person behind is "driving" with lunge lines.

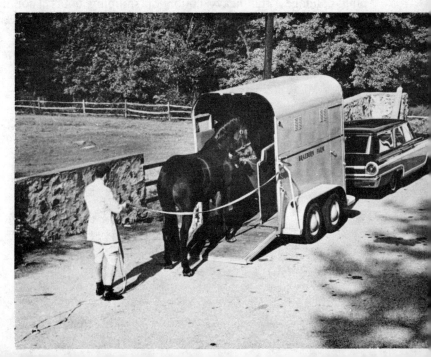

to keep his head down. The assistant should "drive" the horse on with two lunge lines. He can then guide and urge the horse forward by taps with the ropes. Parking the trailer along a fence or wall will keep the horse within the area you want him. Sometimes the biggest problem is to make the horse take the first step onto the ramp. Then the person leading picks up the foreleg and places the hoof in position while the assistant prevents the horse from backing. After a few successful trips a horse that is not frightened will load without the help of the lunge lines.

The body of most vans is higher off the ground than that of a trailer so the ramp is substantially steeper. Therefore it is wise when possible to drop the ramp on a bank thus easing the angle of ascent. Load the horse in the same manner as you would on a trailer except that you should not need the lunge lines as most vans are equipped with guard rails along the ramp. Then the assistant walks to one side of the hind-quarters and encourages the horse when necessary by light taps with a whip. When a horse has been loaded a few times he will walk right on if he just sees someone behind him. Shipping bandages and heavy cotton or shipping boots (not in illustration) will protect the horse's legs from injury.

Chapter XIII

Leads to Hunting

Good sportsmanship is important during casual riding and it is essential in foxhunting, showing or Pony Club. The essence of good sportsmanship is consideration for your fellow riders and for your horse. Think before you act. When riding with friends, don't canter off without warning—their horses will want to follow. You are just asking to be kicked if you ride close to or brush by the horse in front of you. Think too of your horse. Is the footing bad? Is he tired? Never roughhouse while riding. You know what startles or annoys your horse and your friends; be a sport and don't do those things.

Before hunting, check your tack with particular care for worn or cracked places. Make sure all equipment is properly fitted. Note the horse on the left: the hunting breastplate is attached through D rings on the front of the saddle and the sandwich case is attached to D rings on the back.

Foxhunting centers on the fox and the hounds. The riders follow the hounds to see how successfully they can find, hunt and account for (kill or put to ground) their quarry. The hounds hunt the fox by scent which comes from a gland in his pads (feet). The riders enjoy the music (tongueing) of the hounds and the contest between them and the fox. A "Tally-ho!" rings across the countryside; a fox has been found! Will they lose clever reynard as he crosses roads, streams, plowed fields and works his way through thick brush? Will they overshoot the line when he zigzags through open pasture land? Can the "field" keep up with the hounds when they run through wire fences or swamps?

The meet

Moving off

The huntsman helps the hounds with their job. He takes them to a covert where he thinks a fox may be lying. He encourages them when they have "found" and helps them back to the line when they have lost it. The whippers-in help the huntsman by making sure the hounds obey his orders, watching for the fox when he "breaks covert" and by keeping the hounds off deer, house dogs and anything else that might distract them from the job at hand. The master of hounds leads the field. He is the link between the huntsman and hounds and the members of the hunt.

This is foxhunting. The older members of the field do not appreciate the younger generation when they interrupt the sport. Don't chatter when hounds are working nearby and don't run the risk of turning a fox by separating yourself from the field. Stay behind the master and you will get the most fun out of the sport. Strive constantly to save your horse's strength. Don't jump fences unless you must, and stand in your stirrups when going up hills. Never go at a faster rate of speed than necessary. If your horse is hot, keep him moving during checks.

The night before hunting your horse and tack should be clean and your schedule for the next day set up to allow plenty of time to arrive at the meet a few minutes before hounds move off. In the morning feed your horse one hour and a half before leaving, give him a final polishing and have a good breakfast. If you are hacking, ride no faster than a trot and keep out of any coverts you know the hounds will draw. At the meet greet the master and pay the capping fee which helps support the hounds to the secretary if you are not a regular subscriber.

During the day stay alert and watch your hunting manners which insure your own safety and that of your neighbors. Warn the rider behind you of dangers such as holes by saying "ware hole" or pointing them out with your hand; tell him of a quick stop by saying "hold hard" or holding your hand at shoulder level. Tie a red ribbon on your horse's tail if he kicks and keep him away from the others whenever possible. When you have a refusal, let the entire field go ahead before you try again and always give the horse in front enough room to make a quick stop or an error particularly at fences. If your horse is acting up or is pulling and you cannot hold him, leave the field as you have become a nuisance and possibly a menace. Sometimes the master, the staff or some tail hounds must work their way through the field; turn your horse's tail away from them in case he might kick and alert your neighbor by saying "master, please", etc. and "ware hound". Juniors should stay in the back of the field but they need not keep behind an adult who obviously wishes to keep well back or who is having trouble with his horse.

Enjoy your hunt fully by learning the huntsman's calls with horn and voice; watch the hounds work while drawing and casting as well as running. Keep a sharp eye at all times for a fox and if you view one the staff has not seen, face in the

Going on during a run out foxhunting.

direction the fox is running, stand in your stirrup and raise your hat. When you are in a position where you cannot be seen, cry "tally-ho" IF the hounds are not already running or IF they are having trouble working the line and you feel it is the hunted fox. Otherwise, note carefully where you viewed and tell the master or huntsman as soon as possible without distracting the hounds. They will act appropriately on the information.

At the end of the day, thank the master and the staff if they are not too busy, loosen the girth and ride home slowly. When you arrive at your stable, allow your horse small amounts of tepid (slightly cooler than lukewarm) water, check his shoes and give him a thorough cleaning. Should you leave before the hunt is over do so quietly and keep away from any coverts the huntsman may still want to draw.

Chapter XIV

Showing and Pony Clubs...

Do you like to compete? Then you will find that showing is lots of fun. Experienced people will give you their opinion of your horsemanship and the performance of your horse. Go to several shows before you start showing yourself. Watch and learn from experienced riders. Try to judge the classes yourself and then see how your judgment compares with that of the judges.

Get an experienced person's help in preparing for your first shows. Your horse's mane should be braided and, if possible, his tail as well. Your tack and your horse should be shining. Start at the little shows and enter classes that you think you can do well in. Don't enter a 3-foot-6-inch jumping class when you know you or your horse is not ready for it. No miracle is

Braiding the mane.

going to occur the day of the show. School your horse at home, not on the showgrounds! Be a good sport. Don't complain about the judging. Remember: you came of your own free will to get the judges' opinion. However, don't be afraid to ask for the judges' comments on your performance. At most shows either the judge will tell you personally or you will be given cards on which remarks are written.

You will benefit by joining the American Horse Shows Association, Inc., 527 Madison Ave., New York, N. Y. if you are planning to do any substantial amount of showing. Even though you are not yet ready for competition in recognized shows you will learn a great deal from the rule book

This is a nice type of young conformation hunter. Small ears and a kind eye mark his head; his neck and body are well-balanced; the wither is long (running well into the back) and the shoulder long and sloping though both are yet under-developed; the forearm is wide and well placed under the shoulder; the knee is large and clean cut; the cannon is relatively short compared to the forearm, dense, straight and well defined; the fetlock is clean cut and wide; the pastern is strong with a good length and angle; the chest is deep; the back is strong and a good length in proportion to the rest of the horse; the croup is long and sloping and the tail is well set; the thigh and leg are wide and long; the hock is set low in his leg and is wide and well defined.

containing the standards for all divisions and you will receive an interesting monthly magazine, HORSE SHOW.

The AHSA recognizes shows, judges and show officials that meet certain requirements. It admits individual members on the payment of a nominal fee and these members are eligible for certain classes and yearly awards offered by the association.

As a member of the Pony Club or any similar organization you have a definite responsibility. Whether hunting, showing or hacking you carry the honor of the club with you. A property owner may not know that Sue Smith or John Jones rode across his wheat field or his lawn, but he will know that "a pony-clubber did it." Any bad sportsmanship will reflect on your club as well as on you. Be on time for your meetings. You don't want to have to gallop your horse a couple of miles when he still has a day's work to do at the meeting plus his hack home.

What should you wear while riding? It depends on the weather, the job you are going to do and what you can afford. One thing every rider needs is a hard hat, either a hunting cap or a derby. This is an essential protection and you should wear it at all times even if you are not planning to jump. Whatever

Mare and foal shown in hand in a breeding class.

clothes you buy should fit well; ill-fitting clothes can be so annoying that they are dangerous. They are unattractive as well.

Jodhpurs, either wool or cotton, are suitable for every phase of riding. If you insist on wearing dungarees for everyday riding, then make sure they are long enough to prevent rubbing and tight enough to prevent wrinkling. However, if your legs are chaffed easily, you are foolish to wear them; you cannot grip properly with sore legs.

Never wear shoes without heels as you run the risk of having your foot slide all the way through the stirrup. Obviously jodhpur boots are the ideal things to wear with your jodhpurs but laced shoes are suitable. If you do not have a hacking (tweed) jacket for winter wear, then see that whatever you do wear is not so loose or bulky as to interfere with your riding.

The young lady to left is dressed in formal wear suitable for juniors out hunting or showing: black cap, white stock, black coat, canary breeches, black boots with patent leather tops. The young lady in the center is dressed more informally but still suitably for a junior hunting or showing: black cap, colored stock, tweed coat, buff jodphurs and jodphur boots. The young man to the right is dressed correctly for summer showing and cubhunting: black cap, tie, white linen coat, buff breeches, leggings, and high laced shoes.

Formal hunting attire which is suitable on formal days out foxhunting and in classes at horse shows which require appointments. The lady member is wearing a hunting silk hat with a hatguard, a white stock fastened horizontally with a plain gold safety pin, a cutaway black coat with the collar in the livery of the hunt, a yellow vest, leather gloves, buff breeches, black boots with patent leather tops, tabs sewn on and bootgarters, regular hunting spurs, and she is carrying a light hunting whip with thong. The gentleman member is wearing a hunting silk hat with a hatguard, neckwear same as the lady's, scarlet frock coat with collar in the livery of the hunt and brass buttons, white breeches, black boots with brown tops and white bootgarters to match his breeches, and he is carrying a regulation hunting whip. The bit on his horse's bridle is sewn in as required in appointment classes. Also required in AHSA appointment classes but not shown in the photograph: Rain gloves carried under the girth, each on its appropriate side, thumbs against palm of glove and against saddle, fingers toward front of saddle; sandwich case and flask (separate for gentlemen, combined for ladies) containing a suitably wrapped sandwich and a beverage of the rider's choice.

Any member or subscriber may be asked to wear the collar in the colors of the hunt and the hunt buttons. To be asked to wear pink or the hunt collar is a privilege and so you mustn't wear them until you have been asked to do so. Either string or leather gloves are suitable. If you wear a tweed coat you should have brown boots or jodhpurs and brown jodhpur boots. Spurs are optional.

When showing, wear the same clothes as for hunting. However, in the hot weather it is best to wear a summer-weight coat and an abbreviated stock. You may also wear a tie or a riding shirt with a string tie of the same material.

Your riding clothes need not be expensive but they should fit well. After you have stopped growing buy the best clothes you can afford; they are a good investment.

Stand your horse up alertly while waiting for the judges' decision or for a ribbon even though the horse is not being judged for conformation. Remember that your manners and general appearance are always noted although the actual class is over.

Small pony at a trot during a pony hunter hack class.

Large pony jumping in winning style on his way to the championship at the National Horse Show held in Madison Square Garden, New York.

A representative of Argentina on his way to capturing the trophy for an international fault and out class. Notice his flawless form over a big spread fence.

The horse is making a big but apparently effortless jump suitable for a hunter trials or outside course. It would probably be considered too bold for any class in the ring with the exception of a corinthian class.

A young rider with an excellent seat and perfect hands in an AHSA open class, part of the USET combined test finals in New York.

Welsh and Shetland ponies make wonderful driving as well as riding ponies. Pictured: Welsh roadster pony to bike. In this type of class the driver wears stable colors just as in a race.

Green working hunter displaying the style which won him the championship at one of the world's largest outdoor shows: the Devon Horse Show in Devon, Pennsylvania. Note that the rider has lost his hat. In Pony Club competitions the rider should retrieve his hat if lost and his performance will not be penalized.

Chapter XV

And Makes You a Horseman.

Some people ride because they love horses. Others ride to exercise, to get off in the country and enjoy the freshness of a spring day or the colors of the autumn foliage. Some ride for the love of sport: hunting, racing, showing. Many people ride for all of these reasons.

We have given you the basic principles of riding and ways in which to apply them. As in all sports there are several different ways to do many of the things connected with riding. Some methods are better than others. As you progress, you will discover various combinations of aids to use, let us say, in turning or breaking on a lead. You will learn to adapt the management of your horse to his personality. Some horses need a firm hand; others need patient coaxing.

Always keep an open mind about your riding. There is no miraculous set of rules that you can memorize and depend upon to answer every situation. If there were, riding would lose much of its excitement and fun.

Never become discouraged. You can ride well if you really want to do so. For many centuries everybody rode, not only athletes and sportsmen. Horses provided the chief means of transportation. After all, if the fat Wife of Bath and the scrawny Reve could make the long journey to Canterbury, you too can ride!

However, the better your horsemanship and sportsmanship the more you will enjoy your riding. Make the most of your lessons. Listen to the talk of knowledgeable people; question your veterinarian and horseshoer. Have a sense of adventure and ride many different horses. They all have something to teach you.

Are you willing to learn? Then welcome, horseman!

Glossary

action: the manner in which a horse moves his legs i.e. high action, low action, springy action, etc.

aids: rider's weight, legs, voice, and hands

azoturia: stiffening of the hindquarters where the muscles of the loins become tense and hard; often caused by idleness and overfeeding. Treatment: keep horse quiet, cover with blankets, call vet

babble: a hound babbles when he gives tongue for no reason or on scent other than fox.

behind the bit: refusal to accept the bit resulting from lack of impulsion or over-flexion

billet straps: straps on saddle to which girth is attached

blank: hounds draw a blank when they fail to find a fox in a covert

brush: fox's tail

cadence: the regular rhythm of a gait.

carriage: the posture of a horse referring particularly to his head

cast: hounds cast or are cast by the huntsman when looking for the lost line of a fox

cavesson: halter-like equipment particularly designed for lungeing; also sometimes used as an alternate term for the noseband of the bridle.

check: when hounds lose scent out hunting and must cast around in one place for line

cold-blooded horse: one that is not pure thoroughbred

colic: pain due to causes arising in the digestive tract; horse lies down, nips at his flanks, shows obvious signs of pain. Chief causes: bad feed, overfeeding, feeding when horse is hot or excited, eating an excess of spring grass, apples, snow. Treatment: give colic medicine, keep horse warm and walking slowly; call vet

colt: male horse under four years old

couple: the method of counting hounds by twos refers to them in couples, i.e. "twenty couple (forty hounds) out today"; also the name of the equipment used to attach two hounds together

crop: rigid portion of hunting whip; called a crop when used without thong and lash

cry: term applied to the sound made by a pack of hounds while running a line

cub: a young fox

cubhunting: also called cubbing refers to the early part of the foxhunting season before the opening meet and the formal season; this period of several weeks is used to educate the young foxes, hounds and horses

dock: bone of horse's tail

draw: hounds draw an area when they are hunting for a fox; also the area itself may be referred to as a draw

dressage: the advanced mental and physical training of a horse beyond the basic skills of his particular field

earth: a place, usually a hole, where a fox lives (den) or seeks protection

enter: hounds are entered when they start to hunt regularly and are referred to as the entry, i.e. "last year's entry", "this year's entry"

flexion: the giving in the poll and/or the jaw by the horse on instructions from the rider's hands while still accepting the bit; a horse that bends the middle of his neck or gets behind the bit is not flexing properly.

field: followers of hunt other than the master and staff

filly: female horse under four years old

forearm: area of the foreleg between the elbow and the knee

forehand: part of horse in front of saddle

founder: disease of the foot affecting blood vessels and tissue; horse becomes very lame; chief causes: overwork in relation to condition, improper cooling out, improper feeding. Treatment: soak hoofs in cold water, call vet

gait: the various ways and speeds in which a horse moves his legs, i.e. walk, trot, canter, etc.

gelding: castrated horse four years of age and over

gone away: the fox has gone away when he leaves the covert

hack: refers to a horse who performs mainly on the flat; a horse is a good hack that will go alertly but quietly across country but not necessarily jumping; when a rider says he is going for a hack he usually means he is going for a quiet, casual ride

hand: unit of 4 inches used in measuring the height of a horse from the withers to the ground; ponies are 14.2 hands (58 inches) or under; horses are over 14.2

hay belly: also grass belly; a swollen and sagging belly caused by too much forage and not enough work; a horse should be worked slowly until his condition improves

heaves: serious respiratory disease indicated by noisy breathing through widely distended nostrils and a "heaving" belly particularly after galloping

heel: hounds running the line of the fox the wrong way (backwards) are said to be running heel

hindquarters: part of horse behind saddle

hold hard: one rider's warning to another to stop, usually quickly

hunter: a horse particularly suited to foxhunting that shows a steady disposition along with good jumping ability and way of going; this term is never applied to the rider

hunting whip: crop with thong and lash attached

impulsion: the mental desire to go forward transmitted into a physical drive which should animate all of a horse's gaits

jumper: a horse whose main job is to jump high fences; this term never refers to the rider

lash: (cracker) a short piece of knotted cord attached to the end of the whip thong which accounts for most of the noise in cracking the whip

lift: the huntsman lifts the hounds when he carries them forward from a line they are working, probably not too successfully, to a point where the fox has been viewed or where he believes it may have gone

line: the trail of scent left by the fox

lunge line: long rope used to exercise horse from the ground *over reaching:* the horse's hind legs over reach and strike the front legs; usually from lack of impulsion but often can be helped by corrective shoeing.

mare: female horse four years old and over

mask: head of fox

meet: the place where the hunt assembles to begin the day's sport

near side: left side of horse

off side: right side of horse

ratcatcher: informal attire worn at some horse shows, for hacking or cubhunting

riot: deer, cats, dogs, etc., that the hounds might run but should not

school: to school a horse means to work him with certain objectives in mind; you should school your horse in something every time you ride him even if it is only a more alert walk; sometimes used to specify working over fences

stallion: mature horse

steeplechase: race over fences

stern: the tail of a hound

take-off: point at which horse leaves ground in negotiating a jump

thong: The long braided leather portion of a hunting whip

United States Pony Clubs

Abington Hills	Abington, Pa.
Air Force Academy	Colorado
Alamo	San Antonio, Texas
Albermarle	Albermarle Co., Va.
Annapolis	Annapolis, Md.
Arlington-Fairfax	Arlington, Va.
Atlanta	Greater Atlanta, Ga.
Bainbridge Island	Bainbridge Island, Wash.
Bath	Akron, Ohio
Bedford County Hunt	Southern Virginia
Berks	Reading, Pa.
Blue Hills	Los Gatos, Calif.
Blue Ridge Hunt	Boyce, Va.
Brandywine Hounds	Chester Co., Pa.
Bridlespur	St. Louis, Mo.
Bridlewild	Gladwyne, Pa.
Cahaba	Shelby Co., Ala.
Cardinal	Matthews, N. C.
Casanova-Warrenton	Warrenton, Va.
Cedar Hills	Maury Co., Tenn.
Chagrin Valley Hunt	Gates Mills, Ohio
Charleston	Charleston, S. C.
Charlotte	Charlotte, Vt.
Cherry Creek	Cherry Creek Valley, Colo.
Chesapeake	Wicomico Co., Md.

Chestnut Ridge Hunt	Chestnut Ridge, Pa.
Chicago	Chicago, Ill.
Claymore	Columbus, Ga.
Clearwater	Clearwater, Fla.
Colorado Springs	Colorado Springs, Colo.
Contra Costa	Contra Costa Co., Calif.
Cottonwood	Tucson, Ariz.
Cumberland	Cumberland, Md.
Deep Run Hunt	Richmond, Va.
Delaware	New Castle Co., Del.
Elkridge-Hartford Hunt	Monkton, Md.
Evergreen	Seattle, Wash.
Fair Hill	Cecil Co., Md.
Fairfield Count Hounds	Fairfield Co., Conn.
Forest	Bryan, Texas
Fort Worth	Fort Worth, Tex.
Fox River Valley	Barrington Hills, Ill.
Frederick	Frederick, Md.
Fredericksburg	Fredericksburg, Va.
Fresno	Fresno, Calif.
Garrison	Garrison, N. Y.
Genessee Valley Hunt	Avon, N. Y.
Glastonbury	Glastonbury, Conn.
Golden's Bridge Hounds	Golden's Bridge, Conn.
Granby	Granby, Conn.
Green Spring Hounds	Glendon, Md.
Griffin	Williamson, Ga.
Groton	Groton, Mass.

Harts Run Hunt	Pittsburgh, Pa.
Highland Run	Humphrey Co., Tenn.
Howard County	Howard County, Md.
Huntingdon Valley Hunt	Huntingdon Valley, Pa.
Keeneland	Lexington, Ky.
Kingwood Fox Hounds	Flemington, N. J.
Lake Oswego Hunt	Portland, Oregon
Lakeville	Lakeville, Conn.
Lance and Bridle	Hanover Co., Va.
Limestone	Manlius, N. Y.
Lio Lii	Oahu, Hawaii
Litchfield	Litchfield, Conn.
Lone Star	Travis Co., Tex.
Long Run	Louisville, Ky.
Los Altos Hunt	Palo Alto, Calif.
Low Country	Yemassee, S. C.
Loudon Hunt	Loudon Co., Va.
Meadow Brook Hounds	Long Island, N. Y.
Mendon	Monroe Co., N. Y.
Miami Valley	Cincinnati, Ohio
Middle Tennessee	Nashville, Tenn.
Middleburg-Orange County	Middleburg, Va.
Middletown	Middletown, Del.
Midland Foxhounds	Muscogee Co., Ga.
Millbrook	Dutchess Co., N. Y.
Mission Valley	Kansas City, Mo.
Monadnock	Monadnock, N. H.
Monmouth County Hunt	Monmouth Co., N. J.

Montgomery	Montgomery Co., Ala.
Montpelier	Montpelier, Vt.
Mt. Kearsarge	Warner, N. H.
Musketaquid	Concord, Mass.
New London	New London, N. H.
Norfolk Hunt	Dover, Mass.
Normandy Park	Seattle, Wash.
Oak Brook Hounds	Naperville, Ill.
Oakland County	Birmingham, Mich.
Old Chatham	Old Chatham, N. Y.
Oro Madre	Amador Co., Calif.
Palm Beach County	Boca Raton, Fla.
Palmetto	Spartanburg, S. C.
Penobscot	Penobscot Valley, Me.
Pickering Hunt	Chester Springs, Pa.
Pine Tree	Skowhegan, Me.
Piscataquis Valley	Dover-Foxcroft, Me.
Platte Valley	Littleton, Colo.
Plum Creek	Littleton, Colo.
Ponkapoag	Canton, Mass.
Potomac	Potomac, Md.
Presque Isle	Aroostook Co., Me.
Purchase	Purchase, N. Y.
Raccoon Valley	Des Moines, Iowa
Radnor Hunt	Malvern, Pa.
Rainbow of the Foothills	LaMesa, Calif.
Rapid Creek	Iowa City, Iowa
Redland Hunt	Brinklow, Md.

Rolling Hills	Long Beach, Calif.
Rolling Rock Hunt	Ligonier, Pa.
Rombout	Salt Point, N. Y.
Rose Tree	Media, Pa.
Ryder Brook	Stowe, Vt.
Santa Cruz County	Santa Cruz Co., Calif.
Santa Ynez Valley	Santa Ynez, Calif.
Seneca Valley	Poolesville, Md.
Snake River	Lewis-Clark Valley, Wash.
Somerset Hills	Somerset Hills, N. J.
Southlands	Rhinebeck, N. Y.
Spring Valley Hounds	New Vernon, N. J.
Squamscott	Seacoast of New England
Mr. Stewart's Cheshire Foxhounds	Chester Co., Pa.
Tennessee Valley	Knoxville, Tenn.
Upper Valley	Norwich, Vt.
Valley Green	Issaquah, Wash.
Valley Hunt	Bradford Pa.
Vashon Island	Puget Sound, Wash.
Wayne-DuPage Hunt	Wayne, Ill.
West Tennessee	Memphis, Tenn.
Westchester County	Bedford, N. Y.
Western North Carolina	Biltmore Forest, N. C.
Westmoreland Hunt	Greensburg, Pa.
Whidbey Island	Island Co., Wash.
Wilton	Wilton, Conn.
Wissahickon Valley	Philadelphia, Pa.
Woodbrook Hunt	Tacoma, Wash.
Woodlawn	Alexandria, Va.

Index

Percheron, 12
Pony Clubs, see United States
    pony clubs
position of rider, basic, 32-34
        at a walk, 42-44
        at a trot, 49-50
        at a canter, 54-55
        jumping, 71-74, 78-81
posting, 49-52
punishments, 65-68

quarter horse, 13

rein(s), position of, 33
        direct, 43
        leading or opening, 44
        bearing, 43-44
rewards, 66-68
riding lessons, 13-15
running away, 61

saddles, 25
        placing of, 27
scratches, 19
shoeing, 90
showing, 101-103
shying, 67-68

side saddle, 38-40
sitting trot, 51-52
Sloan, Tod, 16
sportsmanship, 15, 97, 99
standardbred, 13
stirrups, adjusting of, 31
stopping, 46, 61-63

tack, 21-22
        kinds of, 22-25
tacking up, 27-29
Thoroughbred, 13, 67, 89
thrush, 20
timing, 52, 74, 79
trot, 49-52
turning, 43-45

United States Pony Club, 14-15, 104-105

vanning, 95
voice, 47

walk, 41-44
walking horse, 13
weight of rider, 42-48, 72-74
whip, 36